Lynn Datrow

with Salt & Sass ♥ *Lynn Datrow* (signature)

ALIGNED
as f★ck

Transforming
*your inner assholes**
into allies

*LIKE ANXIETY

Year of the Book
135 Glen Avenue
Glen Rock, PA 17327

ISBN: 978-1-64649-261-9 (paperback)
ISBN: 978-1-64649-264-0 (ebook)

To protect confidentiality, names and identifying details have been changed or are composites of multiple clients.

While I am a Licensed Clinical Professional Counselor, this content is not intended to provide mental health treatment and is not a replacement for the therapeutic relationship in psychotherapy or the coaching relationship. Always seek the advice of your own Medical Provider and/or Mental Health Provider regarding questions or concerns you have about your specific health or medications, herbs or supplements. If you have or suspect that you have a medical or mental health problem, contact your own Medical Provider or Mental Health Provider promptly.

Printed in the United States of America

DEDICATION

To my mother who
modeled moving forward,
no matter what.

To my husband who
kept his eye rolling to a minimum
and offered encouragement
along the way.

To my daughter who
took it upon herself
to stop my spinning over the cover art
for this book by creating a design
that inspired the one you are holding in your hands.

CONTENTS

No Means No, Not Maybe
No Judgment
No Excuses
Aligned Action

Chapter 6 "E"

Embrace the Process
Embarrassment Won't Kill You
Enter Humor, Stage Left
Aligned Action

Chapter 7 "D"

Discern
Decide
Deal With It
Aligned Action

Salty Language Disclaimer

Considering the title of this book, a disclaimer may seem unnecessary; however, here it is anyway...

Be Aware:

I use Animated Adult Language and I sprinkle it liberally, so if you are not interested in Salty Language, are offended by it, or are in the vicinity of someone with whom sharing it is not appropriate, close this book now and walk away.

SERENDIPITY

Several years ago I met a lovely older gentleman at a training, the kind of person you might refer to as a "character." I don't know about you, but I am drawn to characters. In general, we human beings love stories, and the best stories have a cast of interesting characters!

No surprise then, that I found myself connecting with John. He was a shaman and he didn't believe in coincidence, though he had his own word for it: *co-inky-dinky*! This is a fun way of taking notice of the things that happen to us that seem random, and yet are not. These are things that cross our paths and we choose to notice and even take action... the things that make us say, "Hmm..."

The other day I received a message from my sixth-grade teacher. We are "friends" on Facebook (of course), and it turns out, he is currently teaching a continuing education math class to the 55+ crowd in which my mother-in-law is a student. Jokingly I shared that I don't believe in coincidence, but did wonder about the "odds" (my feeble attempt at a math joke) of this connection. This very logical math-minded man concurred that not only are there no coincidences, but that the odds of us connecting in such a myriad of ways is actually much less astronomical than we might think!

Serendipity rolls off my tongue a little easier than *co-inky-dinky*.

One serendipitous event that moved me in the direction of writing this book happened during a "Book Adventure" at a local independent bookstore. My daughter had been invited to a birthday party for a friend. This whole parenting thing sometimes baffles me, and buying birthday gifts is in the list of top five things I would rather not feel obligated to do as a parent! So I got what I'm going to call "creative." (You can call it chicken shit or lazy if you like, but I choose "creative.")

My daughter made a card and included the following:

> Your gift is a 'Book Adventure'!
>
> My mom will talk to your mom.

Now that may sound all fancy and shit. It's not. My daughter is an only child and we do not live in a neighborhood. When we are at home, she tends to be up my ass to play with her. I'm not actually proficient in the art of play. Picking up an extra child on Friday afternoon after school is actually a win-win. My daughter gets to practice her social skills, and I get some peace and quiet!

So we arranged the Book Adventure, which simply meant that I picked them up from school and drove downtown to our city's wonderful independent bookstore, The Curious Iguana. Once there, the girls were left to wander and ponder their purchases, while I was free to peruse the rest of the store. Within five minutes I felt that familiar tug. A book was calling me from the shelf.

If you have never wandered the aisles of a bookstore and had a book (or books) call to you, stop reading now; you are not my people! Wait, I'm totally busting your chops here. You are welcome to keep reading, though I highly recommend you go on your own Book Adventure and see what happens. There is no feeling quite like that of Serendipity Speaking from the Shelves!

The book that jumped into my life that day is called *The Monkey is the Messenger* by Ralph De La Rosa. Like so many other books that have come to me recently, I received another message of validation.

Why does validation seem so important? Because I have a very loud VoD (Voice of Doubt). This VoD wants me to play it safe and keep my thoughts, feelings, ideas, and experiences to myself. Perhaps you have experience with your own VoD. Mine tells me no one wants to hear my stories or ramblings. It tells me I don't know what I'm talking about. It wants to protect me so much that it sometimes feels like it is suffocating me in the process.

Opening *The Monkey is the Messenger* and reading about "three categories of relationships" (boss, enemy, and ally) was similar to what I have been saying about Anxiety and VoD for years. I confidently closed the book and announced to my VoD, "I do know what I'm talking about and it's time to share my story."

So by whatever serendipitous occurrence that led you to this book, here we go. Let's get ALIGNED as F*ck!

CAST OF CHARACTERS

"Who Are You?"
– just me asking a question...
definitely NOT quoting a famous song!

As I considered writing about the cast of characters I refer to as Inner Assholes, a song (that shall not be named because you can't legally quote the lyrics to songs in a book without permission) popped into my head. Probably because this is the chapter where I want to clarify Who (your clue) this book is for and Why (not a clue) I'm taking the time and energy to write it, my brain apparently thought this would be a funny reference. If you have never heard this song, Google it. It will be much funnier that way.

In some ways I already know the answer to the question that this famous chorus poses. Who are you? You are an enigma. Your inside does not match your outside. You are a Responsible One, an over-doer for others, often at the expense of yourself. You may come across as having your shit together, but inside you see the whole thing as more of a shit show. Maybe you call these Inner Assholes "Anxiety" or "Fear" or "Inner Critic" or "Worry" or "Doubt" or "Impostor," but in any case there is a solo act, a trio, a quartet, or maybe even a fucking Flash Mob in your head that calls the shots... and they are often, if not always, assholes about it.

Why am I writing this book? Because I've been there.

Somewhere in my past I remember seeing a flowchart of research about how we learn best. There was a certain percentage of information retained as you read something, another percentage if you hear information, and a higher percentage if the information is both seen and heard. The point I'm getting at is that the best way to make information your bitch is to teach it to someone else.

That's my goal—to take all of the years of my own journey and share them with you, to educate, inspire, and entertain you in such a way that you too will have a different and better relationship with your Inner Assholes by the time you finish this book.

Let's start with the introduction of some important characters. I've already referenced them. They are a merry little band of fuckers who take their cues from the Grand Poobah: FEAR.

To be clear, I'm going to start where you are, which is feeling like Fear runs the show a lot of the time (if not always). My goal for you is for that specific belief to be much different by the time you and I reach the end of this book. We are going to do some Belief Relief! That sounded fun since it rhymes. What it means is that we will relieve you of beliefs that aren't working for you and maybe create some new ones.

Before I introduce the members of FEAR's gang, I want to share a little history. Fear really does play an important part in our show. It is the leader of a gang of would-be Protectors who feel responsible for keeping you alive. They believe they are in charge of your survival.

If you are reading this they have done their job. Each of your ancestors stuck around on this planet long enough to procreate. Their band of Protectors did their job. That is their goal, their purpose, their mission: to keep you safe and alive.

Here's where the story gets interesting, though. In the last 100 years or so, in developed countries most of the population does not deal with true survival (life or death) situations on a daily basis. Despite our evolution we each still get this merry (or scary, if that feels more like your inner assholes) band of protectors who don't know what to do with themselves. Just like a working dog (think Border Collie here) that is not assigned any work, FEAR and its band of Protectors have learned to just make shit up to give themselves something to do. (Kind of like a working dog herding your kids or chewing on your favorite shoe.) Lucky you to be on the receiving end of their shenanigans.

Let's make some introductions:

Chronic Worry

No matter how much reassurance you get from others, or that you give yourself, there is always another "What if...?" that leaves you with the number one goal of "making sure" and triple checking ALL.THE.THINGS... ALL.THE.TIME.

Anxiety

This asshole loves to pair up with the others to convince you that your main two goals in life (and work) are to be: 1) Certain, and 2) Comfortable. Anxiety is tricky because sometimes it is actually giving you signals that can be helpful, but other times is just nasty noise. It is bossy and insistent and shows up at the least convenient times—like in the middle of the night or right before an important presentation or performance. If it's really digging in and being persistent, Anxiety may have you convinced that the only safe thing to do is... nothing. No risk-taking when Anxiety is in control!

VOICE OF DOUBT (VOD)

"Are you sure?" Since you can't actually be sure of anything (Certainty is an illusion, which we will cover in more depth later) the answer is "No," but that doesn't sit well when your VoD is cranked to 11!

The Inner Asshole that keeps you from stepping into your purpose and power, VoD chips away at any and all signs of confidence and empowerment. Statements like, "Yeah, they said they liked it, but they were probably just being nice" and "You should have done this instead of that" are the sand they use to make you feel as if your foundation is constantly shifting. VoD is also the asshole that keeps you over-doing because its message is that nothing is ever enough!

INNER CRITIC

This asshole's mantra is "You're not doing it right," spoken with whichever accent makes you cringe. Mine tends to sound like a very judgmental and pious old biddy. The Inner Critic tells you that everything must be done "right," but no matter how well or "right" you do the things, the Inner Critic just harps on how not good enough you are. There is no satisfying this one.

IMPOSTOR *

"They are going to figure out that you are a fraud." Once that insinuation gets stuck, you keep waiting for the Impostor Police to show up at your door and cart you away. No matter what evidence there is to the contrary (i.e., how smart and successful you are), the Impostor wants you to believe it is all a fluke.

---

*Funny thing about feeling like an Impostor:

Actual frauds don't spend time worrying about being a fraud, so if you do worry about being found out, it just means that you have an Impostor in your Inner Asshole gang… and that you are, in fact, competent!

Now that you know the names of the characters, let's head to the stage...

INVITATION

> ## Alignment:
>
> *a position of agreement or alliance*

When a new client walks into my office (or their face shows up on my computer screen in this virtual world) one of the first things we talk about is how their challenges appear. Across the board I hear responses that make Fear, Anxiety, Worry, Stress, and Doubt out to be quite the Assholes.

Judge Judy, Debbie Downer, Bitchy Brenda (or Joey the Jerk, Biff the Bully, and Richard the Dick, for you guys) are just three of a myriad of inner critical voices that can show up solo, together like a Dixie Chicks trio, or maybe even, when the situation is particularly overwhelming, like the fucking Mormon Tabernacle Choir!

It can be exhausting to listen to all of their opinions and endless chatter!

In most cases clients beg me to help them get rid of the Assholes. It is at this point that I have to break the news to them that Fear, Anxiety, and the rest of the gang aren't going anywhere. They are part of a built-in survival system. There is no getting rid of them. Then I share the good news... we can teach the Assholes better social skills!

It is during this conversation that I also ask if, while in the throes of a panic attack or overwhelm, anyone has ever suggested that they "calm down" or "just breathe." One hundred percent of the time they answer "yes!" Then I ask the million dollar question... "Does that make you want to punch the person in the face?"

With an emphatic second "YES" and a look on their face that is a mix of surprise and relief, we begin the process of understanding... understanding that I know how their Fear and Anxiety work... understanding that being told to "calm down" and "just breathe" don't even come close to being helpful when Inner Assholes (like Anxiety) are running the show... understanding that they are in the best place to begin the process of taking back control from the Assholes.*

> *OK, they may not understand that last one just yet, but I do! Even if they are not yet fully comprehending how this is going to work, clients share that they feel more confident and hopeful that their quality of life is going to get exponentially better!

At some point during that first session we usually talk about techniques and strategies they have tried with another counselor or on their own. This is almost always an interesting conversation. So often other counselors encourage clients to tell their stories (sometimes over and over again), then reassure them, and teach them mindfulness and meditation, suggesting modalities like Yoga or other ways to relax.

Now, I want to be clear. All of these approaches have value, and I am not suggesting otherwise. I am suggesting, in the words of one very wise client, "There is something before mindfulness!"

Yes! That is my message and the Why behind my writing this book.

When it comes to dealing with your Inner Assholes, to be successful, you have to deal with the "something before mindfulness" before any of these wonderful modalities and techniques can be helpful.

So if you have ever judged yourself to be lacking because you don't meditate "right" can't even get yourself in the room to do Yoga (or want to run screaming right in the middle of class), get stuck in the details of your stressful story without relief (and with a lot of self-judgment), and avoid thinking by overdoing for others, I invite you to join me in getting ALIGNED as F*ck by transforming your Inner Assholes into Allies!

How to Read This Book

I've been doing this work for more years than we are going to count and have so much knowledge and experience accrued. When it is mixed with my excitement it is easy to overwhelm a new client. I often joke that if I could find a way to open up a client's head and pour in all of that wisdom and experience at one time, I would. Since no one has figured out how to do that (yet), it is important for us to pace ourselves. The same goes for the information shared here. Digest it at a pace that works for you.

While I kept to the letters of the word ALIGNED in writing this book, there is no requirement that you read the chapters in strict order. I would suggest that you start with the first chapter "A," though after that you may choose to skip around. Do the Action Steps after each chapter or save them all up to the end. Again your choice.

If you haven't figured it out yet, your Inner Assholes might attempt to sabotage your reading of this book by telling you that there is a "right" way to approach the reading and action steps inside. While I would recommend reading in order, you have my permission, if you need it, to do it whatever way works best for you!

CHAPTER 1
ALIGNED STARTS WITH "A"

"When we pretend that we can avoid vulnerability
we engage in behaviors that are
often inconsistent with who we want to be."
—BRENÉ BROWN, *Daring Greatly*

Here we are, you and I, starting our journey to becoming ALIGNED, and I have an urge to assume that you have already acknowledged your cast of Inner Assholes—those inner parts of yourself who make your life (at a minimum) uncomfortable and (at a maximum) unbearable. However, we all know what happens when we assume, so let's talk about Acknowledgment.

ACKNOWLEDGE

> "But the thoughts are really annoying (overwhelming, scary)!"

Fuck intrusive thoughts. While we are at it... fuck intrusive feelings too!

I'm not disagreeing that your Inner Assholes are, well, assholes. I am going to encourage you, though, to change the way you react and respond to them. It's time to change your relationship with... yourself!

Getting ALIGNED with your Inner Assholes (by turning them into Allies) starts with Acknowledging that they are present, and that they aren't going anywhere... even thanking them for their service. Yes, you read that correctly. You are going to thank them for their service!

Your Inner Assholes have a job. That job is to protect you. They are brilliant at this job, but they are overzealous. They wind up protecting you from perceived threats rather than real ones. As annoying as that is, it is still important to acknowledge and thank them for their service.

Your IAs are there to protect you... they're just overzealous.

Way back before I ever became a parent, I worked with kids in a variety of settings. A concept that really hit a home run for me was learning how to tell a child that their behavior was undesirable, while still conveying that the child was not their behavior, so they did not feel rejected or, at the core of their being, "bad."

Let's apply this here. Your Inner Assholes are the parts of you that have been labeled as "bad." They believe they are bad so they just keep doing what they always have been doing, which is overprotecting you in some fucking annoying and even scary ways... but just like with kids, how you react or respond can make all of the difference. (There is a difference between reacting and responding!)

Rather than reacting with "OMFG, what the fuck is wrong with me? I must be crazy!" and then pushing them away (aka rejecting them), what might your life look like if you instead responded with "Hey, it's you again. Thanks for all of your hard work at protecting me. Now it's time to get back to _____(fill in the blank with whatever your Inner Assholes are distracting you from doing)"?

Yeah, yeah. If it were just that simple, there would really be no point in the rest of this book. What if, though, through a series of simple steps, one building on another, you could actually respond differently and ultimately take back the power from your Inner Assholes and actually be in charge of your life? (Notice that I did not use the word "control.") Awesome, right?

Before we take the next step, let's clarify the difference between *reacting* and *responding*.

Reaction comes from your survival system and is immediate and impulsive. *Response* involves a more thoughtful process and takes just a moment or two longer than a reaction. Your Inner Assholes, since they are all wrapped up in your survival, enjoy it when you react. They find it very entertaining. Part of your transformation into becoming ALIGNED with them will be to stop being an ever constant source of entertainment. You are not their puppet anymore!

ACCEPT

Almost every client has, at some point, watched me pull Elizabeth Gilbert's book *Big Magic* from the shelf and read her story called "The Road Trip." The gist of this story is that once the author realized that "Fear" and "Creativity" were conjoined twins and she made lots of space in her life for Fear, she was better able to partner with her Creativity. When she would begin a new project, there was a little speech she would deliver to her Fear, telling Fear that it will always be along for the ride but not allowed to touch the radio... and positively forbidden to drive!

After acknowledging that your Inner Assholes are along for the ride and that you don't have the option of tossing them out of the car, Acceptance is the next step in getting ALIGNED with your Inner Assholes and converting them into Allies!

Accept that your Inner Assholes are socially-awkward, pain-in-the-ass, lying bullies! Also Accept that they are along for the ride whether you like it or not... Also Accept that *you* have the power to *change* your relationship with them.

Getting ALIGNED will shift your Inner Assholes out of your driver's seat and into the backseat where they belong! That's an appropriate place for your Inner Assholes to hang out. Then you work out a system for them to send you signals of actual danger, without all of the extra noise!

Let's just pull the bandage off here, folks! There is no "getting rid of" Fear, Anxiety, or your vicious VoD (Voice of Doubt)—that part of you that keeps pretending you are an Impostor. All of your thrashing about and struggling only get you buried deeper in the quicksand. We have dark parts, parts that are angry, shame-filled, and fearful. We are told to hide them... and to hide from them. Fuck that!

Behaving as if they don't exist or "shouldn't" exist is a major part of why they can so easily fuck with you! Accepting yourself, part and parcel, the whole kit and caboodle, the whole enchilada... is what starts the change in your relationship with Anxiety and all of the other Assholes. Come on, if you knew that someone wanted to take out a hit on you, would you be super cooperative with them?

What, exactly, are you afraid of?

Human beings fear being wrong, uncool, uncouth, dismissed, rejected, not enough, abandoned, embarrassed...

So many of these hit hard below the belt. If you are "woo," this term refers to our base, our core, our root chakra. If you aren't "woo" (which is totally fine) I am talking about basic needs, like Abraham Maslow's Hierarchy—safety, and social and emotional "needs," aka the stuff we seek to reach the pinnacle of self-actualization!

Let's consider this for a moment. We humans strive toward self-actualization by working hard to get our basic needs met *at the same time as* a band of assholes tells us to do shit (or to not do shit) that keeps us stuck believing we aren't good enough, or telling us we are in almost-constant danger.

Why not train your IAs to help you instead of getting in your way?

What if what's really going on is that you have a band of protectors who have not been properly trained to do their job? If you could accept this and then begin a rigorous training program to teach them social skills and a way to more effectively protect you, how do you think that might change your life?

Maybe you would spend less time catastrophizing (freaking out) and more time considering what you want to do (rather than "need" to do) and focusing on your priorities. You know, those things that will actually lead you to self-actualization?

Acceptance is the hardest part of this process. That's why I started there. (That, and the fact that ALIGNED starts with A.) Acceptance is also the most fundamental and important part of this process. You can attempt to Avoid it, but that would just be another Asshole distracting you.

Behaving like a friend or cousin with terrible insecurities who lacks social skills, your Anxiety and VOD want your sole attention. If they can keep you rapt in their distracting bullshit, then you aren't taking risks or being vulnerable, thereby making their jobs harder. Keeping you safe is easier if you aren't actually living your life!

So how do you actually do this "acceptance" thing?

Excellent question!

Start by changing the story you tell yourself.

At any given moment you are telling yourself that you want whatever is going on to be different. That is your first mistake. (Fortunately mistakes are just opportunities in disguise, so we get to use this as a place to start.)

Look, you don't have to like what is going on to accept it. Acceptance does not mean rolling over and being a doormat. It does mean that you acknowledge that you do not have control over what is going on, but you *can* deal with it. Liking something and dealing with it are not mutually exclusive.

Acceptance does not mean rolling over and being a doormat.

Back when I was just a run of the mill generalist type of therapist, I attended a CE (continuing education) workshop by a man named Reid Wilson. The topic was Treating the Anxious Client (or something like that). Honestly, the bar on my expectation meter was quite low as I have been to some boundary challenged and boring workshops, but Reid was a breath of fresh CE air!

He started the day by making it crystal clear that he was the presenter and that questions were to 1) be held until specifically identified times and 2) better be relevant to most of the audience. How did he motivate the crowd of 100 or so people to cooperate? He threatened to publicly shame anyone who didn't respect his boundaries. This got my attention!

Then about an hour or so into his presentation, Reid had technical difficulties and out slipped one of my favorite words, "Fuck!" It was full-on fan-girl for me from that moment on.

I spent most of the day on the edge of my seat, nodding as I heard strategies and techniques that made so much sense to me. He shared that Anxiety lies to us. It tells us that our main goals in life are to be Certain and Comfortable.

Have you noticed that every advertiser and marketing professional out there must know this about us? Why do you think their products or services are made to help us feel Certain and Comfortable? Just the thought of that makes me facepalm!

Here's the deal. Anxiety is part of our basic survival system. It does have a job and it takes that job seriously. The trouble comes when we treat it like a boss or an enemy. It is neither.

This is the Acceptance part. Accept that your Anxiety is neither your Boss, nor your Enemy. At the same time, you also must Accept that it's not going anywhere.

When you were growing up, did you ever have to spend time with a strange cousin or maybe a neighbor? You know the type. They are socially awkward. If you had a choice (which, because you were a kid, you often did not) you would have blown them off to hang out with your "cool" friends. But since you were forced to be around them, you (mostly) figured out how to deal with them. Sometimes, if it was just the two of you, you might even have gotten glimpses of how they weren't "that bad." Of course if this cousin or neighbor had to share your attention with anyone else, well that's when it was apparent just how socially awkward they really were. Your Inner Assholes behave in much the same way.

They want to protect you and they want you to make their job easier. That's why they work so hard to convince you to hand over control for *all* of your impulses and to take absolutely no risks! This is where it is important for you to Accept that Anxiety isn't going anywhere. You cannot annihilate it or even separate yourself from it. Here's what you can do. You can Accept its presence *while* teaching it better social skills!

When you take back your power, your Inner Assholes begin to fall in line. When you step up to be the Boss and make the decisions, then your Inner Assholes get to go back to being employees, their intended role from the beginning.

Another important concept I learned from Reid Wilson was how us Anxious folks love to get caught up in our content! We love a great story and with those stories comes all sorts of "reasons" we use to justify our Anxiety and restrictive anxious behaviors. Guess what? Our content is irrelevant. Yep, it does not matter!

Now before you toss this book aside with a look of horror, hear me out! I have spent countless hours listening to people's stories. Truth be told, I came out of the womb destined to be a counselor. As far back as I can remember, people would say, "You are such a good listener" to me. (Sometimes to a fault, like when a close friend was reading what a high school boyfriend wrote in my yearbook and asked, "Were you his girlfriend or his therapist?" I like to think I had a lot of life practice before I ever decided to listen to people for a living!)

So I've heard lots and lots of stories. And I've heard lots and lots of bullshit excuses. Don't get me wrong. What happens to us, our stories, are important *and* they get us into trouble when we over-focus on the story rather than our next step.

> *It's time to treat your IAs like employees, not your boss.*

Going back to acceptance, it is in our best interest to Accept that we are drama queens and that the stories we tell ourselves about how we are not competent or strong enough will keep us stuck every.single.time! Accepting this about yourself allows you to get out of the quicksand! (Did you know that it's not the quicksand that will kill you? It's actually your struggle against the quicksand that gets you in trouble!)

Accept that the feeling of panic, the intrusive thought, and the chronic worry all suck. Also Accept that you are much more competent at dealing with those crappy thoughts and feelings than you ever thought you were!

Have you ever seen *The Wizard of Oz*? Looking back, that was some trippy shit, but there is so much to learn about yourself and your Inner Assholes from that story.

Think about it. We spend a good chunk of our lives being told what to do. There is always someone older and more "experienced" willing to tell us what we "should" and "should not" do. Whether it's our parents, teachers, religious figures, or even our older siblings, it's pretty easy to grow up assuming that others know more or "better" than us.

In *The Wizard of Oz*, all of the Munchkins tell Dorothy that Oz is all-knowing and will have her answers. How do they know this? Because it is what they have been told... and they have chosen to believe it. Deep down we are all a little freaked out about being 100% responsible for ourselves, so giving our power over to others can feel "safe."

Dorothy and her motley crew go on their adventure in an attempt to find answers. They jump through hoops and have to be persistent to get an audience with this all-knowing Oz. The hoops just perpetuate the illusion that Oz is Certain! When they eventually meet Oz, the volume really ramps up (just like our Anxiety). Booming voice, fire, freaky floating head. Yeah, that will get your adrenaline flowing.

So they get in front of Oz who tells them they have an assignment. If they do something, then he will give them what they want (which they think will make them feel Comfortable). Off they go to face those fucking flying monkeys and get the witch's broom. Having completed their task, they return only to have Oz say, "Well, now you have to do this other thing too."

Just about the time that Dorothy starts to flip her shit, Toto (leave it to the Little Dog) pulls back the curtain to reveal that Oz is none other than a short little con man with great special effects. Yeah, that about sums it up for your Anxiety. It's a con. It is not all-knowing. It is not the boss. *It is also not your enemy.*

ANTHROPOMORPHIZE

On the first day of first grade, I got lost. Not the kind of lost that includes actual danger (I was still in a school building surrounded by mostly competent adults, basically "lost in plain sight"), just the kind that makes an impression. Inner

Assholes enjoy impressions. They devour impressions like candy!

I loved school. I had been to preschool a few days a week and to half-day Kindergarten prior to entering first grade. Learning came easy to me and I loved the praise and validation that adults showered on me for being so "smart." I just knew that first grade was going to be super cool.

My teacher was a nice young woman just starting her career who turned out to also be my neighbor. She even came to dinner at our house once, but I digress (get used to it).

The morning went well in the classroom. It was time for lunch. The class went to the (what seemed at the time) huge cafeteria and we were let loose to navigate the lunch line and find seating.

Now I don't know if what happened that day led to some kind of lunchroom reform where all the students in one class had to sit at the same table with our teachers or their designees. What I do know is that on that day, a small group of us who had packed our lunch found a table and commenced eating and chatting. We sat there for a very long time. We were first graders having our first experience in a cafeteria, so what did we know? Eventually an adult noticed that our little band of first graders did not look like the older students who were now enjoying their lunch time.

Here's where the "impression" was made. The adult scolded us for not being where we were supposed to be (out on the playground). Interestingly, none of my table mates internalized that impression the same way I did. I guess I was special even back then. (You are laughing right now, right?)

What did this "impression" end up looking like in my life? I cried... a lot. I cried at home. I cried at school. A friend I have known for close to 50 years likes to tell the story of trying to cheer me up by telling me that she liked my shirt, and I snapped at her to "Shut up." My Anxiety, being the protector that it is, was not about to let anyone get close to me!

My daughter discovered an old doll at my mother's house that brought these memories back to the surface. The story behind the doll was that when I was in first grade my school bus driver was my father's cousin Nancy. We used to visit her parents' house and I would play with this doll that belonged to her. Nancy was one of the adults who was getting tired of all of my crying, so she bribed me by offering me the doll if I would stop crying on the bus. My daughter later dragged that doll everywhere when she was little, and we even named it Nancy!

At first, the way my parents and the school dealt with my challenges was for my mother to come to school with me and volunteer in the classroom. After a month with no improvement on my part, this plan was determined to be unsustainable. What I understand now is that no amount of reassurance will make Anxiety go away! If anything, reassurance actually reinforces the anxiety. Reassuring someone just feeds their fear!

So my mother and I had a chat with the school psychologist who suggested I might have Separation Anxiety. I don't know that I was formally diagnosed, I just know that to help me learn to be more comfortable being separated from her, Mom started taking me to the mall and would have me go to different parts of the department store to get things for her. (She could see me, but I didn't know that.)

Wow, all of these extraordinary measures became necessary because my brain took the impression that I had done something "wrong" by getting "lost" in the cafeteria, where I "shouldn't" have been on one day when I was five years old. Fucking Anxiety!

Kind of crazy how our brains work and how well-meaning reassurance can't get Anxiety to back off. (We will come back to this!)

Using this five-syllable "A" is how I ultimately started dealing with my Anxiety in a way that put me in the driver's seat, demoting my doubt and transforming Anxiety from Asshole to Ally. I anthropomorphized it!

Anthro-what? Yes, I know, before I started using this term with clients, I had to literally practice saying it out loud. It's quite the tongue twister. Whether you can pronounce it easily or not, the meaning is the important part.

> ## Anthropomorphize:
> *to put human characteristics*
> *to non-human entities*

Basically I used it to put a face to the fucker, Anxiety. When I discovered the power of Anthropomorphizing my Inner Assholes, I chose to visualize my Anxiety like the green monster from the Mucinex commercials. He is a big blob of snot that behaves like a bully. He moves into your lungs and sets up shop, convincing your body that he's in charge.

That's what Anxiety and your other Inner Assholes do. They move in, take over, and convince you that they are your

Bosses. If you haven't already gotten the memo, they are not your Bosses. They are a band of protectors who are overdoing their job, overstepping their bounds.

In Michelle Obama's book, *Becoming Michelle,* she shares how difficult it was to get used to having the Secret Service in her life. She struggled with them bossing her around until one day it dawned on her that they were actually her employees. After that, instead of approaching situations like she was asking them for permission, she told them what she wanted to do and allowed them to figure out how she could do what she wanted as safely as possible. Michelle Obama is a leader and you can be a leader when dealing with your Inner Protectors, too!

Over the years clients have shared that their Inner Assholes have showed up like Dementors from *Harry Potter,* critical relatives like pious and bitchy Aunt Busybody, the stepmother from *Cinderella,* Slimer from *GhostBusters,* Bogarts from *Harry Potter,* or The Bogeyman. One client simply refers to her Anxiety as "Angie" and frequently rolls her eyes at Angie's antics.

The form is not as important as the characteristics. Getting to know your perceived enemies is the best way to defeat them! Notice that I said "perceived." We are calling them your enemies or Inner Assholes, but let's be clear. *They are a part of you and are not going anywhere.* This is the news that has the potential to send clients running out the door and for you to throw this book against the wall. (No client has actually run screaming from my office.)

When I was a kid I loved the movie *Parent Trap.* (To be clear, I am talking about the original with Hayley Mills rather than the remake with Lindsay Lohan. Yes, I'm that old). It blew my mind how one actress could play her own twin. I still think the camp director was brilliant for throwing the two squabbling campers together in an isolated cabin to work out their differences. Even if they hadn't turned out to be identical twins (yes, this movie did require a heaping helping of suspension of disbelief) I think the concept is sound. Imagine yourself being thrown into a room with your Inner Assholes where you can figure out more about each other so that you can learn to get along!

WALKING THE TALK IRL (IN REAL LIFE)

Acknowledge. Accept. Anthropomorphize.

Amber had done the work to acknowledge and accept her Anxiety, and on the day that she entered my office having done that week's Action Step to anthropomorphize her Inner Assholes, I knew something had transformed for her.

For a little background, Amber was one of my first "ideal" clients—a Responsible One who appeared to have her shit together on the outside, but pulled back the curtain on her inner shitshow during our sessions. We acknowledged her High Functioning Anxiety, a super loud VoD (Voice of Doubt), a judgmental Inner Critic, and a fear that the Impostor Police would be showing up any minute. Amber's merry little band of Inner Assholes left her exhausted from worrying, procrasti-cleaning, fearing that "something bad" might happen, and struggling to fall asleep with all of their "What if's..." constantly swirling in her mind.

Amber valued humanitarian needs and was a social justice champion. She cared deeply about equity, but worked in a field that talked the talk, but did not walk the walk. Amber was determined to affect change there; however, her Inner

---

Assholes (in their pursuit of protection) gave her constant messages that eroded her confidence and held her back from pursuing the platforms necessary to be a leader in her field. When I first mentioned the word "purpose" she shared that it made her feel like puking!

Fortunately, Amber was willing (most days) to do the uncomfortable work of talking back to her Inner Assholes and taking the action necessary to move forward. I mention "most days" because, like all of my clients, talking about their Inner Assholes' shenanigans and what action steps to take while in the safety of my office is more comfortable than actually talking back and taking action in the real world. On that particular day Amber shared that she had named one of her Inner Assholes "Amanda." This was the part of her that insisted that everything had to be done "right" while also giving the message that no matter what Amber did, it wasn't "good enough." Through the work that we had done, Amber was able to see Amanda's value as an Ally: she was the one who encouraged Amber to do her best, but, typical of our Inner Parts when they are behaving like Assholes, Amanda took her job too seriously and had Amber convinced that she was the Boss.

Amber recognized that she had to make a change in how she related to these Inner Parts. It was time to make a transformation. What Amber shared next had me nodding and fist pumping (and there may have been an audible "YES" emitted from my mouth): Amber thanked Amanda for her service over the years, encouraged her to retire, and then sent her on a vacation!

Once this change in Inner Leadership occurred, I observed Amber step more fully into opportunities (rather than make excuses why not to) to use her position to affect the change in her industry. "Amanda" became more of a consultant and Amber began taking cues from her own Inner Wisdom or Inner CEO instead.

SUMMARY

It's Action Step time. Did you really think that I was just going to compassionately share all of this information and not kick your ass to take action? Oh, come on, I'm the Compassionate AssKicker. Of course you are going to get Action Steps.

Do them or not. It is your choice, but the only thing I will offer you later, when you start to whine about this process not working, is cheese!

You are a doer, so I know that you know how to take action. I also know that doing for others feels easier than doing for yourself. If you have to trick your responsible mind by saying this action will benefit someone else in your life, then do that. Whatever it takes!

To review:

Acknowledge that Inner Assholes like Anxiety, Voice of Doubt (VoD), the Impostor, and the Inner Critic are actually a band of protectors who need guidance and leadership from your Inner C-Suite (Competence, Confidence, and Core Self). Just like the Secret Service is not the boss of the First Family, but rather work for them, your Inner Assholes are looking for cues from you as to what you want them to do.

Accept that the struggle is real. Your protectors have been in control for some time and are conflicted about potentially losing their position of power. It's up to you to teach them better skills and give them a clear job description.

Anthropomorphize your Inner Assholes! One of the best tools for doing this work is to visualize your Inner Assholes as having human characteristics. It helps you to understand their motivation and provides a means for you to "talk back" to their demands and negative naggings.

ALIGNED
ACTION STEP:

Choose a name (like Angie or Angus) for your Inner Assholes and/or relate them to a character like the Mucinex Snot Blob, the stepmother from *Cinderella*, or Bogarts from *Harry Potter*... whatever works for you to identify them as entities. Yes, the thoughts and feelings that your Inner Assholes evoke are part of you, but by anthropomorphizing them you separate them enough to change the conversation.

Not so hard, right? One step at a time.

OK, now it's time to watch your Language!

Chapter 2 "L"

"I went to sleep with gum in my mouth and now there's gum in my hair and when I got out of bed this morning I tripped on the skateboard and by mistake I dropped my sweater in the sink while the water was running and I could tell it was going to be a terrible, horrible, no good, very bad day."

— JUDITH VIORST, *Alexander and the Terrible, Horrible, No Good, Very Bad Day*

Alexander definitely had a sucky start to his day, but was having gum stuck in his hair and a wet sweater really worthy of the words "terrible" or "horrible"? When it comes time for a language lesson, I tell clients to save "terrible" and "horrible" for tornadoes and hurricanes.

LANGUAGE

Your Inner Assholes use Catastrophizing Language all.the.damn.time which does not help you to keep what is actually happening at any given moment in perspective. This is one of the most impressive ways that your Inner Assholes stay in control. They use your own language against you.

I "should" be getting more done.

Nope, if you *should have* you *would have*.

Stop "should-ing" on yourself!

>I "need" to "make sure" that a particular thing happens.

Nope, you don't need to do anything except breathe, drink water, and eat food to stay alive. The rest is optional. Remember... you can't *make sure* of anything. That level of control is an illusion.

Do you see where language gets your panties in a wad around a lot of shit that you don't have control over? Yet here you are running yourself ragged by reacting to the language of your Inner Assholes.

Stop it!

If you haven't seen the video yet, do yourself a favor and put these four words into an internet search: *Bob Newhart Stop It*

You will find a videoclip from a MadTV skit starring Bob Newhart as a psychiatrist who practices the briefest of brief therapy with clients. While hilarious and not intended as "real" therapy, he does make a point. If your brain is speaking to you as if it is your boss (either telling you to do something you don't want to do or just generally being mean, negative, or even scary), tell it to fuck off. Replace the thought with something that is more aligned with who you are and what you want to do.

Yeah, I get it. That sounds easy enough, but it's not. Or is it?

Would you speak to your best friend, a child, or a lover (or even a stranger on the street) the way that your Inner Assholes speak to you? If your answer is "No," then Stop It! (If your answer isn't "no" then I don't know if this book is really going to help you.)

If "Stop it" is not enough, see if this exercise will help. Write a letter to yourself from your Inner Assholes. Make it as controlling and critical as they are to you on a daily basis. Now read the letter to yourself as if you received it from another person. Does it piss you off? Good!

Now respond with a letter from your Allies—the parts of you that know you are a fucking amazing person. Get it all in there, counter every last point, and make mincemeat out of the Inner Assholes' taunts and untruths. You would defend your loved ones without question, so it's time to do the same for yourself!

The more work that I have done in dealing with chronic worriers, control freaks, and Debbie Doubters, the more that I notice language emanating from Inner Assholes. It's like nails on a chalkboard where every other word seems to be "anxious speak."

I was once in a van full of other moms on our way to chaperone a field trip. By the time we arrived at our destination I was already exhausted. Why? Because for the entire one-hour ride to the zoo, at least half of the moms in the van were focused on "making sure" they were doing what they thought they "needed" to do, and then questioned whether they "should" do something else instead. Oh, and then the "what ifs?" started. Picture me doing a facepalm right about now!

At first I attempted to help them see how their Inner Assholes were playing them, but they didn't get it. Since I wasn't being asked to share my skills, I shut my mouth and bit my tongue. I hear it every day, though, anxious and critical language that isn't helping the speaker live a life of acceptance, confidence, or ease.

When it comes from clients (and sometimes friends or family) I do go ahead and point it out, since it is what they pay me for.[1] Changing from anxious to empowered language will make a huge difference in your progress toward transforming your Inner Assholes into Allies.

Another word that seems innocuous, but is slowly and subtly eroding your confidence? "Try." When you throw the word "try" into a conversation you are really telling yourself and the other person that you think you are most likely going to fail at whatever you are about to attempt.

If you were sitting across from me right now I would do a little experiment to help this concept sink into your subconscious. Let's see if we can do it virtually. If I were sitting across from you with a colorful ball in my hand and said, "Try to take this ball from me," what would you do? If you took the ball from me, I would say, "You didn't 'try' to take the ball. You *took* the ball." If instead you put your hand on the ball or didn't do anything, I would say, "You didn't 'try' to take the ball. You didn't take the ball."

Don't make me Yoda up on your ass: "Either do or do not. There is no *try*." Yep, "try" is a concept. We use it to set ourselves up to be less disappointed if we fail.

> *Your language may be subtle, but word choice packs a powerful punch.*

Let that sink in. I want you to begin to notice how many times a day you use or hear the word "try." You will be annoyed with yourself (and me). Don't say I didn't warn you!

---

[1] My friends and family just get lucky when I'm feeling generous!

Your language may be subtle, but it packs a powerful punch. Investing the time in being more aware and changing it is well worth the effort.

LEAN IN

> *"I know I should be meditating to
> calm myself down, but I've tried it and
> there must be something wrong with me,
> because I just can't get it."*

I hear this from clients all the time. My response often blows their minds: 1) There is nothing wrong with you; 2) Stop "should-ing" on yourself; and 3) I don't teach people to meditate or breath to calm anxiety, in fact I teach them to wind their Anxiety up and then whip it into shape!

Don't get me wrong. All of those techniques have value, but they just aren't as effective as they can be until you know Anxiety's game and how to play it to win.

Calming techniques end up being more like "False Comforting" techniques. They may help once in a while, but in the end, they lead to frustration when they don't work consistently. Anxiety, when it's being a true Asshole, will eat your breathing techniques for breakfast and use them to leave you breathless (and not in a sexy way)!

Remember when I shared earlier about how well-intentioned loved ones (or just random people on the street) suggest that you "breathe" or, even better, "just calm down"? Something important to consider, before you punch them in the face, is that your anxiety is most likely making them uncomfortable. Their "suggestions" are more about their own discomfort and less about being truly helpful. It sucks *and* it's human nature to seek comfort.

So what do you do about it?

Choose to Lean In.

Remember my reference to *The Wizard of Oz* in the last chapter? The supposed "all-knowing" wizard wasn't satisfied with Dorothy and her crew doing what he asked. Had it not been for Toto's pulling back the curtain, he was going to ask them to do the next task on his never ending list.

Just like your internal fear-based protectors though, no matter what you "do," they are never satiated.

What if you could pull the curtain back on your Inner Assholes and recognize that they are just playing you?

Facing your Inner Assholes with the knowledge that they are conning you—and doing their best to convince you that they are in control—is the most empowering thing you can do for yourself.

If it were that simple, though, all the cool kids would be doing it.

What makes all of this so challenging?

Clients tell me all the time, "Yeah, it makes logical sense when I'm sitting here talking to you..."

Then they throw their big *BUT* into the mix...

"*But* when I'm in the moment of panic or feeling anxious and afraid, all of what we talked about goes right out of my head!"

Excellent observation, grasshopper.

It may seem counterintuitive, but once you lean in, you are going to...

LEAD

When my daughter was about three, my husband hung an image of a toddler wearing both a crown and a frown on our refrigerator. We got a good chuckle. The gist of the picture was about how toddlers are convinced they rule the world.

Two things, though, about this seemingly innocuous joke.

First, young kids do think they are in charge and every adult (or even older siblings, cousins, neighbors, classmates, etc.) does their damnedest to give them the clear message, "You are not the boss of me!"

Second, "with great power comes great responsibility" (a concept that has been quoted for centuries and made most recently popular in *Spider Man* comics), so kids quickly adapt to letting someone else be responsible.

You already have an inner guidance system that knows what to do.

Here's the rub, though. When we turn our power over to others and cling to the belief that someone "out there" is in charge, we forget that we have our own inner guidance system—the part of us that knows what to do in any given situation.

We get so caught up in the idea that someone else knows what we are supposed to be doing that we open the door for Fear and Anxiety to walk in and set up command central.

We become so entrenched in the idea that our parents, teachers, principals, coaches, bosses, and any other adult we interact with are "in charge" that we forget that we are the "boss of ourselves."

We let our Inner Assholes take over and run our show...

...Assuming that whatever they tell us to do or not do is the "right thing."

Yeah, so that idea you picked up in childhood about right and wrong? Let's work on how that may be one of the most important beliefs to kick to the curb!

"What if...?" This is your VoD's (Voice of Doubt) favorite game.

What if I fuck it up?

What if I'm embarrassed?

*What if they figure out
that I don't know what I'm doing?*

What if I fail?

Oh, there is so much material here! Where to even start?

VoD's "What if...?" games are just a means of distraction and control. Remember there is no absolute right or wrong. There is also no linear path to anywhere important. Life is about all of the ups and downs, the twists and turns.

My mother was what was, in the late '60s, considered an "older mom." I laugh at that now. She became my mom at age 26... while I became a first-time mom eighteen days before I turned 43!

Anyway, one part of her being "older" was that most of her and my dad's friends had older kids.

When I was five we went to an amusement park with a few other families. All of the other kids were teens. They had been building up how much fun the rides were going to be, especially the roller coaster. Excitement was mounting by the day.

My mother already knew that she was not a roller coaster person, so the plan was for me to ride this behemoth of a ride with the mother of one of the teens. From what I remember I truly was experiencing all of the sensations in my body as "excitement."

When we got to the head of the line, the other mother and I were directed to the front car. Rather than drag this story out, let's just say that by the time we headed down that first big slope, the other mom was holding me back on the seat as I was doing my damnedest to crawl under it!

I know now that I get motion sickness at the drop of a hill (pun intended), so roller coasters (and flying and anything else with twists, turns, or bumps) are not my idea of a fun time.

Life is like a roller coaster, though. There are parts that make you feel like vomiting. But you can learn to deal with the shitty parts while also enjoying the less vomit-inducing parts.

Learning things about your journey and how your internal family works (especially the Protectors) helps you to be empowered in your journey.

Look, if no one has ever explicitly pointed it out to you, let me be the first: none of us gets out of this alive!

Yes, I know that's a shocker. Part of how your Inner Protectors (Anxiety, Worry, VoD, Critic) control you is to have you either over-think death (and therefore keep you frozen or stuck) or under-think it (and keep you distracted from your true purpose).

Accepting that you have one shot at this wild roller coaster of life *and* deciding to be in charge of it (which is different than being in control) is a great first step in demoting the parts of you that are making it so hard to enjoy the ride!

That is what we are talking about here. Learning that there is a part of yourself—call it your core self, inner guidance, or Inner CEO—that actually knows who you are, why you are here, and can handle anything that comes your way, is a key component to the ALIGNED process.

Are you familiar with your wise mind (Inner CEO, Core Self, Inner Guidance) and where it hangs out? Go find it. I'll wait...

Now that you are aware of this part of yourself, it's time to transition from the Protectors (Inner Assholes) being in control to your Inner CEO taking charge.

Remember how I shared Michelle Obama's light bulb moment about the Secret Service working for her and not being her Boss? It's like that. When you can start seeing your Protectors as working for you rather than being your Boss, well that's a game changer!

Maybe it feels like those Protectors have more information than you do. Maybe it feels easier, safer to just do what they tell you to do, or not do.

Sure, if you want to spend this one precious life of yours playing it safe, pushing yourself to the point of exhaustion, restricting where you go, who you interact with, and what you experience... go for it. Is that really what you are here to do, though? Make it to the finish line unscathed with no great stories to tell? You are the hero in your story, so act like it!

WALKING THE TALK IRL

Language. Lean In. Lead.

Larry was a "should-er" when we started. He was drinking (and had been most of his life) the "Productivity is King" Kool-Aid that Inner Assholes use for fuel. In a little trip down memory lane back to childhood, Larry and I saw a clear path of generational "you are what you do" and "you have to give your all to others" that led to his people-pleasing ways and the loud voices of his Impostor and Inner Critic.

We started with having him notice how often he used words like "should," "try," and "need" as well as the phrase "make sure." It was a lot more than he wanted to admit!

As Larry started changing both his internal dialogue as well as his external ways of communicating with his bosses, subordinates, and even his family, it warmed my heart to see how quickly he was able to more fully step into being a leader rather than an exhausted, frustrated, and even fearful manager.

Larry was one of my Rock Star clients who devoured the resources that I shared and came to each session with his Action Steps from the previous session done and dusted! No longer was he letting his employees walk all over him and he found himself more willing to speak up in Executive Team meetings rather than being a passive listener.

Larry's Inner Assholes are still with him, but he recognizes their shenanigans much more quickly now, has stopped "should-ing" on himself (most days), and is a much more relaxed leader both inside and out.

SUMMARY

Watching your Language is more powerful than you realize. When it is being driven by your Inner Assholes you will spend way too much of your time "making sure" to "try" and only end up "should-ing" on yourself.

Leaning In is one of the hardest concepts in this process. It feels counterintuitive to agitate your Inner Assholes. But it is the only way to let them know that you are no longer going to fight with them or take their shit!

Lead. You got this. Tap into your C-suite and demote the Assholes! They work for you, not the other way around. They may not fall in line peacefully, but they will fall in line. Be consistent and "act as if" you are the boss until you gain the competence and confidence necessary to be in charge.

ALIGNED
ACTION STEP:

Take notice of your fear-based language and see what it feels like to change it up, at least once in a while. This may take time and it will require patience. Just start with awareness and then look for opportunities to make changes.

P.S. There was a bonus action step in this chapter to write a letter to yourself. Did you do that one or did you skip it? You be the leader here and decide if you are going to take advantage of the bonus action step or let it go...

CHAPTER 3 "I"

> **Illuminate:**
>
> *1) Make (something) visible or bright by shining a light on it; light up.*
>
> *2) Help to clarify or explain.*

Your Inner Assholes are the dark parts... the parts that you don't like, that you don't want others to see, and that you would rather not deal with. Except you have to deal with them, because they are part of you. So rather than allowing them to shoot daggers at you from the dark (where you have tried to banish them—unsuccessfully, I might add), let's shine a light into the darkness.

Fear is the Grand Poobah from which all the other Negative Nellies in the Inner Asshole gang emanate. It is also an essential component of your survival system. It isn't going anywhere, but you do not have to be a slave to it or its minions.

The human brain is built to assist the body and soul in surviving. It comes with all of the components and wiring. A bazillion years ago life was extremely hard and survival was the number one goal. Fear would arrive during times of stress and put on a show with one of its responses: Fight or Flight. Either choose to fight the saber tooth tiger or flee from it. Success at either of these two meant that humans stayed alive at least long enough to procreate.

Then humans figured out that they could create ways (and things) to make their lives easier—tools, weapons, shelters that could keep predators out, and shoes to make running away more comfortable. Yay! This served the human species for quite some time.

Up until about 100 years ago, seeking comfort was important for survival. Seeking to comfort your empty belly would push you to hunt or gather food. Seeking comfort in order to keep all of your fingers and toes pushed you to create warm clothing and shelter.

Today most of us do not live under circumstances where we need to be pushed to seek comfort. Our lives are relatively comfortable already. Yet, you may find yourself in an almost constant state of comfort... yet still continuing to seek more and more.

This is where Anxiety shows up. You have an anxious thought, then seek false comfort to rid yourself of the Anxiety and associated uncomfortable feelings. Lather, rinse, repeat. Over and over and over again. Talk about a bad habit. Anxiety has you trained to ask "how high" when it says "jump!"

Remember how I mentioned earlier that reassurance just feeds Anxiety? This is how that Anxious Thought/False Comfort Loop works. You have an anxious thought and then seek reassurance or a way to comfort your system such as working harder, curling up under a blanket, binging your favorite _____ (TV show, podcast, or substance, or other activity), or any other way that you have found to "false comfort" yourself. The trouble is that it is very, very temporary and then you are just off to the races (racing heart) again!

Over the years I have come to describe Anxiety as "the thoughts and feelings that put words to our Fear." It is the part that reacts to the panic button and wants to ruminate on unhelpful thoughts. It can show up fiercely like a panic attack or more subversively with a game of "What if...?"

Anxiety lies to you some of the time, but not necessarily all of the time.

Anxiety is tricky because it lies to you some of the time, but not necessarily all of the time. Reid Wilson makes the distinction between *signals* (when Anxiety is actually doing its job to keep you safe from real threats) and *noise* (when it's just being an Asshole for the hell of it). Learning to tell the difference between the two goes a long way in either bearing the brunt of Anxiety's taunts or being the Boss, discerning whether the ping from Anxiety is signal or noise and responding accordingly.

Doubt (or as I like to refer to it "Voice of Doubt" or VoD) plays its part in this fear-based play as the one who keeps you from being too big for your britches, or to keep you from dying of embarrassment. It can behave as if either of those scenarios is actually possible, when no one has ever actually died of embarrassment... and if you get too big for your britches, well, just get new britches, bitches!

If your VoD isn't loud enough, you may have an Inner Critic. Mine tends to sound like a pious Great Aunt on my dad's side of the family who rivaled Judge Judy for being judgmental and dismissive. When I hear the voice of my Inner Critic, I remind myself that all my Inner Protectors have their own backstory and I don't have to get caught up in it.

People (and our internalization of their voices in our head) are not perfect, no matter how much they pretend or would like others to believe them to be. I do my best to remember that I am Perfectly Imperfect and use that mantra as an antidote to the poison spewed by my Inner Critic.

You can be Perfectly Imperfect.

Anxiety, VoD, and your Inner Critic love to set the stage for one other Inner Asshole, the Impostor. Their messages are full of incompetence (yours, not theirs) and reasons why you shouldn't even bother. Do you believe them?

Wait, you don't think you are capable or competent, even though there is plenty of evidence to the contrary?

Oh, so the Impostor got your tongue, then?

This is the "I" that gets in the way of you confidently saying, "I am..." The "I" that lurks around gazing out your window, expecting the Impostor Police to show up and arrest you for being a fraud. Fucker!

Another way that Fear manifests itself is by mistaking modesty for humility and then taking it a few (dozen) steps too far.

While Impostor Syndrome (also spelled Imposter in the U.S.) is a relatively new term (and not a diagnosable mental health condition), it does affect a large percentage of the population in a variety of ways. Impostor Syndrome occurs in people who are actually quite capable and competent, but who have a very loud Voice of Doubt (VoD), fear they are a fraud, and are just waiting for the Impostor Police to show up at their door and call them out. What really keeps them in this cycle of denying their competence (and therefore having difficulty feeling confident) is a disconnect between their external success and their ability to internalize it.

There are five types of Impostors, and some of us are such overachievers that we fall into more than one category!

So as to not leave you with the impression that one is any "better" than the other, I'm going to share the types in alphabetical order.

THE EXPERT

The *Experts* experience fear around expecting themselves to know "everything." That's a fucking heavy load, my friend. It reminds me of a story I once heard (and looked up again using Google) when Henry Ford sued a reporter for slander. (The reporter had called him an "ignorant pacifist.") At this point in time, Ford was doing pretty well for himself. You could call him successful. He chose to confront this troll in court. The reporter's lawyer was asking Ford some ridiculously complex questions in an attempt to provide the evidence that Ford was in fact "ignorant."

Ford is quoted as replying, "If I should really *want* to answer the foolish question you have just asked, or any of the other questions you have been asking me, let me remind you that I have a row of electric push-buttons on my desk, and by pushing the right button, I can summon to my aid men who can answer *any* question I desire to ask concerning the business to which I am devoting most of my efforts. Now, will you kindly tell me, *why* I should clutter up my mind with general knowledge, for the purpose of being able to answer questions, when I have men around me who can supply any knowledge I require?" The point of this? Stop expecting yourself to be an expert in "everything."

THE NATURAL GENIUS

Then there is the *Natural Genius* who expects everything to be easy, and when it's not, assumes it is an internal character flaw. What is really going on here is that a lot of things come easy to intelligent and competent people... but it is still important to immerse yourself in the learning process. Break tasks into chunks and get to work instead of avoiding anything you think you aren't "good" at and underachieving in the process.

THE PERFECTIONIST

The *Perfectionist* will procrasta-plan until the cows come home and benefits from the mantra "progress over perfection" to move forward. Perfectionism can come from a number of root issues, but emanates from the thought (planted by that over-protector Anxiety) that there is only right and wrong, so if whatever you are doing isn't "right," it would be "wrong"... and then you just get stuck in the swirl of all or nothing thinking. Hello, cognitive distortions!

Learning to talk back to this distorted thinking is a key component in taking back your wheel from the Impostor and internalizing your competence and success rather than looking for external validation for all that you do.

THE SOLOIST

A *Soloist* behaves just like you might think. They act alone. They believe that they are solely responsible. They also struggle to work with others. When they have been part of a group project they will not take credit for their part.

The way to challenge the Soloist in you? Collaborate with others *and* focus on people you have learned from. It takes more than one person to make the world go around!

THE SUPERHEROES

Last, but definitely not least, are the *Superwomen/men...* the ones who expect themselves to excel at every.fucking.thing. They overdo to the nth degree and make those around them look like slackers. What's wrong with that, you ask? It's not sustainable. Superwomen/men are more likely to burn out and even end up in self-harming situations due to their high expectations of themselves.

Damn, that's a lot! Of course not everyone who experiences anxiety or doubt suffers from the impositions of the Impostor. If you do (or know someone who does), what is your next step?

Tell the Inner Critic (one of the many internal manifestations of Fear and Anxiety's bestie) to shut the fuck up. While you are at it, being aware of your tendency to cuddle up with the cognitive distortion of all-or-nothing thinking could help. If I hadn't already completed the first chapter "A," I might be attempted to add "Awareness" because it's pretty fucking important.

You know, since I've already pointed out the importance of awareness, let me take another moment to share that often times Impostor Syndrome is closely tied to High Functioning Anxiety. It's the kind of anxiety that isn't obvious on the outside, but is quite the shit stirrer on the inside.

High Functioning Anxiety (HFA) looks like ambition and success on the outside, but is actually driven by intense fear of failure or disappointing others.

Sound at all familiar?

People who experience HFA function reasonably well (part of why this is not an actual mental health diagnosis) and why they may not even view themselves as anxious. They do, however, experience many, if not all, of the following:

> Overthinking (and overanalyzing) almost constantly
> Fear of failure accompanied by a strive for perfection
> Insomnia and its friend Fatigue
> Difficulty saying "no" and a driving need to please others
> Tendency to dwell on past mistakes
> Nervous habits such as nail-biting, hair twirling or leg shaking

That last one hits home for me. If I've had any amount of caffeine, no one wants to sit next to me. If only I could capture the energy expressed as my legs take on a bounce all their own.

Now might be a good time to bring up how your Inner Assholes use caffeine to trick you. They are pretty convincing about how it makes you more focused and energetic. What they don't tell you is that they feed on it and use it to torture you. I won't get up on my soapbox here, just consider cutting caffeine and see if your IAs notice the difference.

My experience (from within my own HFA body and with clients) is that it's like we do use our IAs to our benefit; however, not so much like Allies who make an efficient plan, but more like a bunch of emotionally charged townsfolk storming the castle with their pitchforks at the ready!

Wondering if you are an HFA? Here are more signs:

Constant thoughts of "What if...?" (You've heard that before)

Avoidance or procrastination that lead to "crunch time," get shit done, swirling dervish moments

Comparisonitis

RDD (Relaxation Deficit Disorder)

Worrying about the future until you actually feel intimidated

No finish line for your racing thoughts

With your standard garden variety anxiety we recognized the age old fight or flight response. With High Functioning Anxiety you may more likely experience two other responses. The one you have heard of would be Freeze. The one that you may be less familiar with is Fawn.

Just like it sounds, Fawning is when people-pleasing is used to feel safe. HFAs often use people-pleasing to avoid or diffuse conflict, feel safe in relationships, and seek the approval of others.

Now that you have a more Illuminated view of your Inner Assholes, let's shift your focus to how to actually teach them better social skills.

INSPIRE

If I said the word "Purpose" would it make you feel like puking?

Too often I have found that people get overwhelmed or stuck in their pursuit of purpose. That may be because, just like searching for a life partner, you let Anxiety lead the search party. Since Anxiety actually wants you all to itself, it's like putting the person who has a secret mad crush on you in charge of finding your soulmate.

So what do we do about it?

Glennon Doyle, in her book *Untamed,* talks about finding your purpose in whatever brings you heartbreak. I love this idea. Whether it is social justice, supporting others going through a similar heartbreak (her example was women who experienced stillbirths coming together to support women at high risk for complications and actually bringing down the incidence of stillbirths in their area), or rescuing animals, the willingness to open your heart to the thing that breaks it—while taking action to make a difference... yeah, that's purpose.

So what does Purpose have to do with Anxiety and Self-Confidence? Oh, my dear, everything!

When you stop letting your Anxiety overdo its job of protecting you, and instead put your Inner CEO in charge of running your show, while pursuing your purpose, you are actually using your survival system for good rather than evil.

Okay, that was just a tad dramatic, which is one way I bring humor into the mix.

Here is a little known secret about Anxiety... it's a drama queen! Have you ever noticed how the words "terrible" and "horrible" get thrown around like confetti? Like I shared in the last chapter, I encourage clients to save *terrible* for tornadoes or tsunamis and *horrible* for hurricanes, hunger strikes, and hate crimes.

Instead of feeling bad about your tendency to exaggerate, this is where you use your imagination to give your Inner Assholes jobs. Put them to work helping you think about the possibilities, both negative *and* positive. Don't let them whisper sweet panic in your ear. Tell them to get to work figuring out how to support you in following your dreams, desires, and purposeful pursuits!

What are the actual possibilities? Rather than getting stuck on catastrophizing the negatives, use the creative genius built into your Inner Assholes to imagine all manner of amazing positive outcomes!

Again, I am purposefully being dramatic when I tell you to use your Inner Assholes' powers for good instead of evil! I understand that it's not that easy to change biologically ingrained and environmentally trained behavior habits (that includes your stinkin' thinkin' habits, too), but this is exactly the place for you to start.

Feeling inspired yet? Then let's light 'em up!

IGNITE

> *"What you wish to ignite in others*
> *must first burn within yourself."*
>
> —AURELIUS AUGUSTINUS,
> Early Christian Theologian

My passion for helping others to change their relationship with themselves started with my own journey. What burns within you? What are your Inner Assholes keeping you from sharing with others?

Let's light the fire that Ignites your passion and fuels a persistence in pursuing your purpose while simultaneously melting the icy grip of your Inner Assholes!

The more aware you are of your Negative Nelly thoughts, the quicker you stop them in their tracks and replace them with more positive and productive ones. Know that thoughts get the ball rolling, so thought changing is an essential part of this process. It is the cornerstone of Cognitive Therapy, and adding Action to the mix gets you some Cognitive Behavioral Therapy.

Since this book is not by any means meant to replace therapy for you, if you feel you need it, I will say that CBT is one of the most researched and well regarded therapeutic methods out there. Is it the only successful one? Nope. It is a powerful one that I have used with great outcomes for myself and my clients. I even bring components of it to my coaching clients as well.

Back to changing your thoughts. I know that it isn't easy, but none of the really awesome stuff of life is truly easy.

Curiosity is important (but alas, it doesn't start with the letter I). When Fear and its minions are putting you through your paces, one way to interrupt the old patterns is to get curious. Take a moment and imagine what your life might look like if Fear (and minions like Anxiety, VoD, Inner Critic, and the Impostor) were not actually in control of your life? Are you willing to let yourself go there?

Before I met my husband I was involved with a nice guy who just wasn't the right nice guy for me. We were in that stage of our relationship where we weren't good together or apart. One day we were having yet another conversation about why our relationship wasn't working. I mentioned feeling tired and that I wanted someone else to be in charge for once. He chuckled and asked, "What do you want the other 90% of the time?" Busted!

One of the many lessons that I learned from that conversation and that "failed" relationship was that it is important for me to both know what I want *and* be willing to do the work necessary to achieve it. Too often we get caught up in being "busy" doing things that don't align with our values and goals. Our Inner Assholes use what I call "overdoing for others" (family, friends, coworkers, bosses) to keep us from taking the risks inherent in pursuing our passions and purpose. We are the only ones who can change both our thoughts and our behaviors and get them ALIGNED with our purposeful pursuits. Be aware, though, that just overdoing or overachieving without intention (and the cooperation of your IAs) will wear you out.

Are you really ready to get ALIGNED as F*ck? Then let's keep going...

WALKING THE TALK IRL

Illuminate. Inspire. Ignite.

Irena was one of many clients plagued by Intrusive Thoughts. Because these thoughts can be deeply fear-inducing and embarrassing, clients often take a few sessions before feeling safe enough to share that they are even having them, let alone be willing to share details about them.

Once Irena shared that she was having scary intrusive thoughts (usually they are of the genre of "something really bad" is happening and you are somehow responsible), I reminded her that the content of her thoughts was actually irrelevant, so she didn't have to share the details.

The way we illuminated the situation for Irena was to dig into the work of "thoughts are not facts." After naming her Anxiety "Izzy" and refusing to let Izzy be in charge, Irena was quick to accept the darker parts of herself by shining a light on their shenanigans and actually dealing with the thoughts and feelings she was having rather than attempting to hide them (or from them).

One of Irena's overwhelming fears was related to being a mother and manifested in some over-controlling and overdoing for her daughter. Once we worked on Irena reframing the situation to how she could give her daughter the opportunity to learn while simultaneously doing her own work of doing less, not only did Irena feel more in charge of her Inner Assholes, her relationship with her daughter improved immensely.

In the time that Irena freed up for herself, she became inspired and took the action necessary to create a course that would benefit a group of women who were underserved. Does Izzy still show up and attempt to play "footsies" with Irena? Of course she does. The good news is that Irena notices Izzy's tricks much quicker and takes the action steps necessary to keep Izzy in her Ally gang rather than letting her cross the Asshole line.

SUMMARY

Illuminate (shine a light on) all of those internal parts that scare and trigger survival shit. Bringing them into the light allows you to work even deeper on Accepting them like we talked about in the first chapter. Knowledge and awareness are powerful tools.

Whether you are connected to your Purpose or feel more like puking at the thought, use the dramatic license that your Inner Assholes share as you continue your journey to keep the process lighter and more enjoyable.

Ignite (or reignite) your passion without letting your Inner Assholes put out your fire. Life is not lived in the comfort zone or a bubble. At the very least, stretch your comfort zone a bit more each day. If you are an overachiever, take an even bigger L.E.A.P. to Lead with Empathy, Awareness, and Perspective!

ALIGNED
ACTION STEPS:

1. If you haven't already named them, here is your second chance. Name your Inner Assholes and tell their backstory. Why are they fighting so hard (with you) to protect you?

2. Notice that they are not nearly so scary in the light.

3. What jobs can you assign them that are helpful to you rather than hurtful?

CHAPTER 4 "G"

GET OVER YOURSELF

I was ready.

> Wake up early ✓
> Do my morning routine ✓
> Quiet space ✓
> Close all the open windows on my laptop ✓

Then I opened my notebook and...

"Fuck, I forgot to..."

There went my Anxiety and VoD, teaming up as usual to toss distractions down on me like monkeys flinging their own feces at the zoo.

So I acknowledged them and then started typing. No buying into the drama and no false comfort. I got over myself and all my "What ifs...?" and got on with the business of getting my writing going. I chose not to react to my Inner Assholes or any of the thousand other things I could be doing or people I could be rescuing.

Now it's your turn. Stop letting those voices in your head (your Inner Assholes) dictate what you do and when you do it.

Yes, it can be really challenging to ignore them. That doesn't mean it's not worth the effort. Allow the Inner Assholes to say their piece and then find your Inner CEO who will set you straight. Like when I was wrestling with things that wanted to distract me from writing this book, reminding me about writing my weekly email (and at least 1000 other things), my Inner CEO said "stick to the plan and pull some great shit out of the book to put in your email later." Thank you, Inner CEO, for offering a possible win-win situation.

But what if the issue is that whatever you are working on is "not good enough"? Bullshit! That's just your Inner Assholes protecting you from embarrassment, and let's remember that no one has ever died from that!

I have worked with so many teens and young adults who are scared shitless about getting their driver's license. I've also used this approach for myself and clients when there is a big-ticket purchase or tough decision about leaving a shitty job, but the client is feeling stuck.

The strategy?

Plan to fail.

Actually, don't just plan to fail, *want to fail*.

I recently shared this concept with an overachieving HFA client who looked at me like I had two heads. "You want me to fail at something... like *on purpose*?" She was not thrilled when I answered her question in the affirmative. A week later when we met again, though, this young woman was eager to share that she had, in fact, allowed herself to purposefully accept the possibility of failing at something... and the world had not come to an end! Clients often end up feeling a measure of freedom they never had before just by opening up to the idea of failure!

By planning to "fail" at even the important things (taking a test, going into business for yourself, or riding out the last wave at a shitty job) and accepting failure as an option, the wind is taken out of the Inner Assholes' blowhole and allows you to get over yourself and move forward.

Oh, did you not know that's how creating works? I don't remember exactly where I first heard this, so my apologies if it came from you... but if you are not embarrassed by your early creations then you aren't doing it right. This also applies to taking tests. No one cares how many times you failed your driving test, except you. Get over yourself.

In graduate school there was a big-deal exam called the Advancement to Candidacy Exam that I ended up having to take three times before I passed. At the time my Inner Assholes were having a heyday torturing me about what a loser I was and how failing this test was going to end my career before it started. Flash-forward 30 years and no one gives a flying fuck about it. I got over myself.

The way to gain confidence is to feel competent. The way to feel competent is to practice. The way to practice is to start taking action. The way to take action is to start with a shitty first draft or first attempt at whatever is staring you in the face!

All of this is about getting over yourself. Stop letting your Inner Assholes make the unimportant into something uber important. I frequently share Steven Covey's "Four Quadrant" method of time management to help illustrate where your Inner Assholes trip you up. Quadrant 1 is for things that are both Urgent and Important. Let's agree that these items on your To Do List get done first.

Where I see most Inner Asshole trickery is that people mix up Quadrants 2 and 3. You get caught up in doing the Urgent/Not Important items before addressing the Important/Not Urgent ones. It seems like a "Duh" kind of thing; however, my question for you to ponder is "Why?" Why is it so easy to get caught up in all of the urgency instead of discerning what is more important?

Because human beings love to get caught up in the drama!

If your Inner Assholes (who are the minions of Fear) are in control, then you are stuck *reacting* rather than *responding*. What do we like about reacting, which typically involves you doing something for someone else? The dopamine hit. Or the adrenaline hit. Both brain chemicals can provide at least a few moments of false comfort. One of the problems with this behavior pattern is that it can become a habit, and not the good kind.

No more false comfort and taking care of others' wants before your own just to get a shot of adrenaline or dopamine! It's time to get over yourself and take the next step.

GET ON WITH IT

I wrapped up a final session with a client that I had been seeing regularly for about five years. As we reviewed her progress she was able to note that while she had understood what we talked about intellectually for the whole time we worked together, one of her biggest challenges had been putting the work into practice regularly. What I pointed out was that she had, in fact, been putting the work into action for a few years and that what she was now feeling was the confidence that had come from those action steps.

This is where I also see the Impostor show up. Clients who are actually taking much more action than they realize, fail to give themselves credit for it. Action doesn't have to be huge. It just has to be enough for you to say to your Inner Assholes, "You are not the boss of me," when they tell you to stop in situations that are not actually life or death.

Fear is part of your survival system. Sometimes your amygdala says "fight" and sometimes it says "flee." Those are the two prompts we are most familiar with. When other factors intervene, you might "freeze." This can look like avoidance. It can look like the inability to decide, so you just stop.

Did you know that there are two other options when Fear is fucking with you? *Challenge,* or *Tend and Befriend.* According to Dr. Kelly McGonigal in *The Upside of Stress,* when we can shift from the old fight-or-flight pattern and instead see the stressful situation as either a Challenge ("how can I do something different and learn from it") or Tend and Befriend (shifting the focus away from yourself to caring for someone else), the stress from Fear is dissipated in a much different way.

The trick is getting your mind and those Inner Assholes to cooperate—reframing the situation from stressful, so you either stop or avoid, to finding the opportunity in the stress.

Do you love mentally masturbating? Just stroking and stroking all of those amazing ideas in your mind?

Hey, I love masturbating just as much as the next person but it's not enough to just pleasure yourself. Humans are meant to interact and share amazing ideas and inspirations with others.

What gets in your way of the next step?

In my experience with millions (OK, maybe a bit of an exaggeration) of mental masturbators, I have found that one of the ways their Inner Assholes get in the way is to keep them stuck in indecision.

You can choose not to decide, but that means you have actually made a choice (paraphrasing a famous line in a famous song that shall remain nameless so that I don't cross the no-no line).

This is what actually makes it kind of funny. You are so busy not deciding that you don't realize you have actually made a choice!

Let that sink in a moment...

You are so busy trying to avoid a decision, you don't realize that your inaction is actually your choice.

Haven't we talked about "try" already? When I hear people say the word "try," I throw up in my mouth just a little. Yoda returns, chanting, "Do or do not. There is no try." You can't fucking *try* to do anything. Either do it or don't do it!

Why make such a big deal of a tiny word like "try"? Because words have POWER.

Now that I've ranted, I have a confession. I still use the word "try" on occasion. I catch myself (or my daughter loves to call me out on it) most of the time and rephrase what I'm saying.

70

Why make such a big deal out of a tiny three-letter word? Because words have power. They impact us both consciously and unconsciously. They can set us up for success or they can set us up for failure.

"Try" is an abstract concept. You can't actually "try" to do anything. So why do we overuse this annoying little word? Because we are afraid we may fail at whatever we are "trying" to do, so we cover our asses. "I'm going to attempt to do this thing, but just in case it doesn't work out, let's not be disappointed, OK?" Fear gets into your head and fucks with you once again.

So let's get back to why not making a decision is still making a decision.

Are you happy with your choices? Joyous, even? I thought not. So why do we make some decisions so easily and others not so much?

There are lots of reasons. And all of their paths lead back to Fear. Some decisions can be easy to make because we have no skin in the game, or because we have so much skin in the game that we back up our desire with action. Maybe you had someone with strong decision-making powers making all of your decisions as a child so you have no practice (which means no competence, which means no confidence). Maybe you confidently made a decision that didn't work out, so now your Inner Assholes show up as second guessing.

The older we get, the more we default to behavior patterns we have run in the past. It's just "what we do."

Here's my question, though. What's the worst thing that could happen if you made a decision and it did not work out?

I was stuck in decision fatigue the first time I went to counseling. (I actually went because Anxiety had me twisted up in some pretty tight knots.) I had recently broken up with a man I once thought I would marry. I was well on my way to being 40, and so afraid that my single status was a neon FAILURE sign to the world, that I had temporarily misplaced my confidence. Thankfully my insightful and wise counselor pointed out that I could make a decision... and then, if the result was not what I wanted, I could simply make another decision. Fucking brilliant!

It is amazing how twisted up we can get ourselves over something that, when we step back and observe, is just not that important. Your Protectors strike again. They can be so great at their job of keeping you safe that they actually don't allow you to live!

So how do you get past the mean and scary things that your internal voices use to keep you from taking action? You reframe what is actually going on.

Remind yourself that when you do what your Internal Protectors tell you to do (or *don't do,* as the case may be), you are making their job easier. They are attempting to take the easy way out. If you are inactive, mentally mastur-bating, procrasti-planning, procrasti-cleaning, or whatever you do when your Inner Assholes have you stuck, they don't have to work very hard to protect you. You are doing their job for them. (Don't do that!)

GO TAKE ACTION

Angry yet? Good! Anger is a very helpful action-oriented emotion. When you find that sweet spot of Action that stops short of aggression, well that's Fear actually working for you!

Say what? Yep! Remember all of the emotions that you have, up to this point, put in the category of "bad" are actually just different manifestations of good ol' Fear. Anger has its base in Fear and, unlike some of its cronies, will push you to take action.

Still struggling with this whole Action thing? You might be saying, "But I'm busy all of the time! As a matter of fact, I'm fucking *exhaustipated,*[2] so don't tell me I'm not taking Action!"

Of course you are tired, but I'm going to point out that you are doing all kinds of busy work for your Inner Assholes and other people. What are you actually doing for yourself?

We could chat about all of this like cows endlessly chewing their cud, but in the end it comes down to you being willing to do the scary thing instead of hiding behind doing everything else, mostly for other people, that you and your Inner Assholes use as a means of avoiding doing the things you dream of doing.

> *You're busy all the time...*
> *for other people.*
> *What are you actually*
> *doing for yourself?*

Whether it was your parents, other authority figures, or just "society" in general that pushed your fear buttons and convinced you that it was not OK to want what you want, *Get over yourself, Get on with it,* and *Go take action!*

I have just thrown a whole lot of holy shit your way. Take a moment to process as much of it as you can. Come back and reread this chapter as many times as you need.

---

[2] *Exhaustipated:* too tired to give a shit.

WALKING THE TALK IRL

Get over it. Get on with it. Go take Action.

Gwen had struggled with both Internal and External Assholes most of her life. A people-pleaser to her core, Gwen had some fairly challenging relationships with her family of origin that she continued to navigate as an adult, on top of having internalized their external voices into her internal gang of Assholes.

While it did not happen overnight, Gwen navigated her way through the twists and turns of transforming her Inner Assholes into Allies. She acknowledged and accepted both her internal and external assholes (mostly in the forms of over-controlling family members) and worked through her survival fears of abandonment and safety. Her Internal Assholes seemed to have just as much tenacity as her external ones!

One day, though, Gwen shared her dream with me—to quit her job (did I mention there was even family drama related to her means of making a living?) and travel the country by camper for a year. Holy shit and hell yes!! So we got to the work of taking this idea from dream to reality.

Gwen is one of my clients who truly walked her talk. Did she take her baggage and Inner Assholes on the road with her? Yep. Did she let them influence her decisions along the way. Sometimes. Did she find ways to "get over it and get on with it"? You bet she did! I was so honored to bear witness to her journey and all of the amazing action steps that she took along the way!

ALIGNED
ACTION STEPS:

In Chapter 4 we moved past the concepts into the realm of Action.

Get over yourself and all of the bullshit you buy into that keeps you from really moving toward being the you that you want to be.

Get on with discovering more about how to get your Inner Assholes to work for you rather than against you.

Go take action instead of mentally masturbating so much. Just be clear that the actions you are taking are intentional and not just more chasing your tail out of obligation or attempting to control others.

Now, identify one thing that you actually want to do (not *need* or *feel obligated* to do) and write out the action steps it would take to put this desire into action.

When the excuses start to pile up, head on to Chapter 5 to learn what to do about that!

CHAPTER 5 "N"

"The ability to say no to yourself is a gift. If you can resist your urges, change your habits, and say yes to only what you deem truly meaningful, you'll be practicing healthy self-boundaries. It's your responsibility to care for yourself without excuses."

—NEDRA GLOVER TAWWAB, *Set Boundaries, Find Peace: A Guide to Reclaiming Yourself*

NO MEANS NO, NOT MAYBE

You're used to being responsible for everyone else and you've heard it said a bazillion times to say "No" to others, so what do you think about this flipped script of saying no to yourself and becoming responsible for your self-care "without excuses"? That's quite a bit to chew on.

Next question (I'm just full of them) is what do your Inner Assholes have to say about this whole "boundaries" thing? My guess, which isn't really a guess since I deal with this both personally and professionally, is that you get some seriously mixed messages from your naysayers.

There was definitely a time when kissing the asses of those in your tribe was actually a fairly important part of staying alive. If you were to piss off the people in power you could find yourself out on your keister and, more importantly, alone. Being alone hundreds and thousands of years ago was, most likely, a death sentence. Surviving by yourself was definitely a lot harder back then.

Fortunately these days if you get booted from one tribe (your family of origin, a job, or a social media group) there is always another one waiting with open arms. Your Inner Assholes, however, did not get the memo on this. They may still be encouraging you to kiss the asses of people who do not actually have the power to sentence you to a life of solitude.

So what is a Responsible One to do about setting and upholding better boundaries? The simple answer is: Pick one and practice it. Just like all of the other action steps we have discussed (that I wrote and you read), it really is as simple as choosing one area to work on (be that acceptance, language, leading, boundaries) and then taking the uncomfortable steps to forging a new habit.

Choose one area to work on, then take the uncomfortable steps to forge a new habit.

Yep, reactions that are rooted in Fear and encouraged by your Inner Assholes are just habits... ways that you have gotten used to responding that are habitual but can be changed. Is it easy? Nope, but then none of the best stuff of life is easy!

However, society is set up to encourage you to prove yourself at work and at home. It's the way to keep the other tribe members happy, so that you get to stay in the tribe. How do you best prove yourself? By being the responsible and competent one, of course. You believe that if you just *Do* for others then it will guarantee peace, love, unicorns, rainbows, and a secure place in the tribe. Your Inner Assholes have deemed this to be true.

But is it?

Are you familiar with Tom Sawyer? He's the guy from Mark Twain's story who was a master at getting others to do his work for him. Do you have any Tom Sawyers in your life? Most Tom Sawyers are not intentionally colluding with your Inner Assholes, but they will take advantage of your fear of rejection and your desire to prove yourself competent.

Is that why you are still doing your teen's laundry, all the work for the group project, and staying up late to meet a deadline because you don't know how to tell a member of your team (for which you are the designated leader) to get their own work done?

In Kim Scott's book, *Radical Candor,* she shows leaders (and this can apply at work and in your personal life) the importance of being direct in your communication with others. Too often us anxious types will default to ruinous empathy (caring personally, but not being direct), but that doesn't help anyone. We may see it as being "nice," and therefore continuing to be accepted in the tribe; however, it is not giving the other person a chance to 1) know what you actually want, and 2) decide if they want to learn from the situation themselves.

Scott encourages readers to Care Personally while also Challenge Directly (being Radically Candid) when communicating with others. Yikes! Did your Inner Assholes just do a double take around that "Challenge Directly" phrase? It's not comfortable. It is imperative, though, that you find your way around this whole boundary and direct communication thing if you want to live your best, more purpose-fueled, and successful (by whatever definition you choose) life.

It's time to practice saying "No" and "Not right now" and maybe even "I have all the confidence in the world that you, Tom Sawyer (aka your child, significant other, colleague, co-worker, employee, etc.), can do this yourself!"

NO JUDGMENT
(AKA... STOP SHOULD-ING ON YOURSELF AND OTHERS)

"But I should do everything for everyone all.the.time," said every Responsible One that I know in some form or another.

Yes, we talked about your habit of should-ing on yourself back in Chapter 2, and I'm circling back to it here because it is one of the main challenges to being ALIGNED as F*ck.

Judgment of self and others is just another way for your Inner Assholes to keep you stuck and spinning rather than finding and pursuing your passion and purpose.

Every client (family member, friend, and random person on my street) has heard me say, "Stop should-ing on yourself!" While it brings a chuckle, people find this a difficult habit to break. Your Inner Assholes love to make you *should* all over yourself.

So how do you stop with all the *should*?

The first step to changing any habit is to notice it. Just spend a day or week spotting how often you (and everyone around you) says the word "should."

The second step is to forgive me for pointing this out to you!

Next, really notice how often "should" actually means, "Something or someone outside of myself has me mostly convinced that this is a course of action for me, but some internal part of me is not 100% on the same page."

Learn that the use of the word "should" is a big ol' red flag waving around and shouting, "You only think this is what you are supposed to do, but it might not be!" Your Inner Assholes, eat "should" for supper!

So what keeps you from making the leap from "need" and "should" to "I fucking want to..." and "Yeah, I choose to..."?

You know the answer is Fear, right? When you are stuck and avoiding something, the reason behind your current status can always (and I do not use that word very often) be traced to FEAR.

FEAR can stand for False Evidence Appearing Real, or False Emotions Appearing Real, or False Experiences Appearing Real, or Forgetting Everything About Reality, or False Expectations About Reality, or probably 20 other acronyms. Just remember that while FEAR feels real, it is not True!

*Remember...
thoughts and
feelings are
not FACTS.*

When you can remember that your Thoughts and your Feelings are not *facts*, well, you can keep the should-ing to a minimum!

When your Inner Assholes are loud and obnoxious, it is easy to get caught up in the shoulds rather than listening to your own intuition and feeling confident in what you know to be yours to do. Being triggered by shoulds is part of your survival system.

Back in the day it was much more difficult, if not impossible, to survive on your own. Making decisions based on the expectations of your family and tribe kept you safe and protected by the group. However, we don't live in the same situation now. Pushing boundaries and questioning the shoulds is what encourages our species to innovate and evolve.

It is all fine and good to say, "Stop should-ing." I know it is not that simple.

You want to belong and you want to be liked and you want to be perceived as "I have all my shit together." So you bust your ass and when you don't do something you think you should be doing, you chalk it up as a flaw, should-ing on yourself once again.

Stop it!

Like it's not challenging enough to have others should-ing on you. Should-ing on yourself is not the icing on the cake!

Now that you notice how many times a day (hour or minute) you "should" on yourself, it's time to stop.

Really look at the thing you think you know you need to do and ask yourself, "Is this true? "

I was first introduced to this concept through the work of Byron Katie in her first book *Loving What Is*. (Yes, her name seems backwards, but that is not a typo.) Byron Katie was having a very difficult time dealing with her overwhelming emotions and all of the shoulds when she hit rock bottom and then found her way back to herself. She developed her approach (called "The Work") and one of the key components is learning to question what you believe to be true, by simply asking yourself, "Is that true?"

This question has become one of the most used in my toolbox. When I have an overwhelming or troublesome thought or feeling, I ask myself if it is, in fact, true or simply a thought or feeling that my Inner Assholes want me to believe as fact.

Just this simple question may help you see that you are holding on to a belief that is not ALIGNED with your internal knowing, your intuition, your core self.

No Excuses

Yeah, I get it. You like to call them "reasons," right? Or maybe valid justifications? Explanations that exempt you from encumbrance?

You can call them whatever you want, but they are still excuses. Just one more way that your Inner Assholes gang up to keep you stuck and spinning.

Bottom line: If you actually, at your core, want something, well, then, you figure out a way to make that thing happen. No.matter.what!

Excuses are one way that we human beings create False Comfort. You are welcome to list off all of your obligations, crises, and out-of-your-control-chaos... yet they are still just excuses.

You might be afraid that actually taking all of the necessary steps to do what you say you want to do will lead to being uncertain and uncomfortable. This is the fuel for the fire that creates the smokescreen that keeps you stuck.

I know you've read a story or two about an underdog who came out on top, such as: Madame CJ Walker (first woman to become a millionaire despite being the daughter of slaves and being orphaned), Bethany Hamilton (champion surfer despite having her arm eaten by a shark at age 13), Jim Carrey (homeless at one point), Oprah Winfrey (abused as a child), Ben Franklin (dropped out of school at age 10 because his family couldn't afford it), Albert Einstein (didn't talk until he was four), Richard Branson (dyslexic), Stephen King (first novel rejected 30 times), J.K. Rowling (*Harry Potter* rejected 12 times), Kris Carr (diagnosed with a rare form of cancer, now an expert in healthy living). There are people every day who defy the odds and do "the impossible." These people are portrayed as heroes.

In case you don't already know this... you are the hero of your story!

Who am I? Well, I'm your guide. Your guru. Your Obi-Wan Kenobi. Your Yoda. Oprah's Gayle or Maverick's Goose. All heroes can use guidance and support along the way.

So how do you stop your habit of making excuses and start moving forward in your hero's journey?

You are the hero of your own story!

By doing it anyway.

"But the kids need me to help with their homework." Do they really, or are you just over-controlling the situation because Anxiety told you it was necessary?

"But my (co-workers, employees, children, group members) won't get it done (right, on time, the way it should be done)." Umm, do you hear yourself?

Take a moment and write down (or look at your already well-curated To Do list) of all the things you think you "have" to do. Now, look at the list and get real. How many of them could be done by someone else?

I'm not asking who would do the best job of executing any of these items—we already know the answer is you. I'm asking which ones can only be done by you?

Yes, one of the examples I am using is specific to women with families. It's on purpose because women with families are the most likely to use the obligation card as an excuse.

When did parenting become an Olympic sport? When did we buy into there being a "right" way to do fucking everything? When did our Anxiety get in the driver's seat and make us into overdoing perfectionists who believe we are responsible for everyone and everything around us?

But this is not just a woman-centered problem. Men use excuses, too.

I have a client who claims that spending quality time with his family is a priority, but who also was (and I say "was" because he is working to change this shit) staying up late doing the work that one of his employees was responsible for yet wasn't doing. When I questioned this disconnect, he was able to observe that the employee was not completing work due to nosing into irrelevant company issues and causing problems rather than doing the work assigned. When my client was able to see more clearly, he realized his desire to be "nice" and take tasks off this employee's plate was only giving this person more time to not do their job and cause problems in the company!

When you do things for other people that they can do for themselves, you are setting both you and the other person up for a bumpy ride.

> *"Never help a child with a task*
> *at which he feels he can succeed"*
> —Maria Montessori

My daughter attends a Montessori school and this is one of the tenets I so appreciate yet have to work diligently to remember (and remind the other members of our family frequently).

My daughter is a bit of a Tom Sawyer. It runs in the family as her half-brother is a bit of a Tom, too. It's like they were born knowing how to get others to do things for them. I do not have that gene. I was born with the Responsible One DNA, or, at the very least, was conditioned to it. What makes life interesting is how easy it is for me to team up with Tom Sawyers.*

> *to be clear, Tom Sawyers can be Responsible Ones too, they have just figured out how to delegate better!

I digress. It is all related, though, so hang on as I circle back to Excuses.

You can keep telling yourself the same old tired-ass stories about how you are too exhausted, stupid, uneducated, unprepared, not good enough, or whatever, but there is someone out there who has a similar situation to yours who has decided to talk back to their Anxiety and do whatever it takes to move forward toward their goals.

How do they do it?

One step is to get crystal clear on what you want and what you value.

Most of the time when a client is claiming they want X and then lists off all of the reasons they can't get X, we discover that maybe they don't actually want X. At least not in the version they are thinking of.

Wow, that was vague!

Here's a more detailed example. You might say that you want to exercise. Nope, you don't want to exercise. Most people don't actually want to exercise. If they did, then gyms wouldn't have rosters of members who only show up between January 1–15. What you really want is to feel healthy, and you think that exercising will get you there. You aren't wrong, so why do you struggle to fit exercise into your day? Why do you make excuses to not exercise?

Mostly because we suck at: 1) identifying what we really want, 2) knowing what we value, and 3) prioritizing.

Mark Manson refers to this phenomenon as "shit sandwiches." We say we want something, but we don't want to deal with all of the crap that it takes to make it happen. Anything worth doing has some amount of poop to scoop. Excuses are a way of skirting around the issue. What you are actually doing, though, is eating a bunch of shit sandwiches that aren't the right flavor. Decide to eat a better flavor shit sandwich that is actually aligned with what you want to accomplish.

But it still isn't that simple, is it?

When you are so entrenched in your Burden of Busy and doing what you feel obligated to do, where do you find time to even start to figure out what you want and what you value?

You make it a priority.

Remember my reference to Steven Covey's matrix in the last chapter? Let's apply it again here (because it's that useful). We all know what tasks are Important and Urgent, but too often the second tier that takes our time and attention are tasks that feel Urgent but are Not Important. It's these Urgent but Not Important tasks (usually being thrown at us by someone else) that we use as excuses to not do the things that are actually Important, just Not Urgent. Sorting this out will help you immensely. When you focus first on Important and Urgent, and then Important but Not Urgent (dropping the Urgent and Not Important), your world will pivot greatly!

Now I wasn't going to say anything about Quadrant 4, but since your Inner Assholes may sometimes encourage you to hang out there for more time than is healthy or helpful to you, Quadrant 4 is where the Unimportant and Not Urgent meet. This is where social media and all other "distractions" live. Sometimes it's tempting to use the excuse of spending time in Quadrant 4 as a "need" to veg out that you want to disguise as self-care. I'm going to call bullshit on that one. There are a lot of ways that you can take care of yourself, and scrolling for dopamine hits on social media ain't it.

One of my high achieving clients who was not only working a 9-5 job, but also kicking ass with her own start-up company, was lamenting about how exhausted she was and how defeated she felt about not winning every competition that her company was entered into. While we were doing the work of cognitively challenging and reframing how most companies don't make it to the top 5 of these competitions regularly like her company was, she also admitted to bingeing *Shark Tank*. Once I pointed out that her Inner Assholes were convincing her that watching this show was "research" when in fact it was "ridiculous," she was able to see where her energy was being drained instead of charged.

How do you charge your battery? If it is with activities from Quadrant 4, no wonder you are still tired!

WALKING THE TALK IRL

No means no, not maybe. No judgment. No excuses.

Many of my clients get up every day and kick serious ass doing work that makes a difference. Whether they choose to do their purposeful work for small businesses or bigger companies, they are attracted to vision and mission statements full of promises to make life better for the planet and the people who inhabit it. Nora was one such client—the kind of employee that is a boss's or company owner's dream, a team player who gets shit done. A Responsible One.

Nora had never considered herself to be anxious. If something needed to be done, she made it happen. Then she started waking up with a weight on her chest and the feeling that she was in a tunnel, with a freight train barreling down on her, and she envisioned her foot stuck in the tracks. Scary shit. When we started working together, Nora's Inner Assholes were not only beginning to impact her ability to focus on work, they were making their way into her relationships at home as well.

Once Nora acknowledged her IA gang and accepted that high functioning anxiety was part of her mix, she worked through some of the other steps fairly quickly. Where we plateaued and spent a bit more time was on boundaries. Nora was stuck in overdoing for others both at work and at home. While she was being groomed to succeed her boss, she admitted to both me and herself that she no longer

---

wanted to do the less creative work of that department. She wrestled with even the idea of disappointing her boss, let alone making the decision to pursue another position within the company or possibly leaving altogether. Simultaneously Nora was still overdoing at home, being both the breadwinner and doing the laundry.

We did the deep work on setting boundaries both at work and at home. (Don't be the parent of the kid who has to figure out how to do their laundry in college). Then came another lesson in not should-ing on herself or others. It was not up to her boss to guilt her into taking a position that did not fit her well. It was not up to her company to tell her that she had to value work over her family. It was up to her to be willing to transform her Inner Assholes into Allies, and it was up to her to be willing to speak up for herself and be willing to look for a company whose values were more aligned with hers.

Long story made short, Nora left the excuses behind (for the most part) and pursued a more creative position of leadership in her company and, last time I checked, was teaching her children to do their own laundry.

SUMMARY

How are you feeling about the little "N" word? "No" is such a small word, but it really does pack a mean punch in the gut!

If toddlers can so easily learn to say no, you can too.

So to review:

No means no. Creating boundaries and sticking to them are essential, not optional, no matter how much your Inner Assholes slap you around about them.

Stop should-ing on yourself. Period.

No excuses—they are just your Inner Assholes attempting to justify their overzealousness at protecting you.

ALIGNED
ACTION STEP

Get out a roll of duct tape and use it on your Inner Assholes. Just kidding (sort of). Maybe a better way to visualize this transformation from Asshole to Ally is for you to give each of the current Assholes a new job description. What are they allowed to do for you? Next, work on enforcing those boundaries!

Now take a realistic look at your To Do list and admit which tasks can truly only be done by you and which ones could be done by either a family member (at home) or a colleague or employee (at work). Boggles the mind, right?

Chapter 6 "E"

Embrace the Process

Last week I let a client into our Zoom meeting and was surprised to see him in casual clothing, including a ball cap, and sitting in what looked like his bedroom. Before I could inquire as to the change of typical scenery and attire, he started chuckling and shared, "I got fired on Tuesday!"

Wait, wasn't he supposed to be upset, anxious, even panicking? Not on my watch. I regularly tell clients to "want" to be fired. As a matter of fact, I had said this very thing to this client a couple of months into our work together.

It's the same as when I tell clients to "want" to fail their driver's test, the Praxis exam, or any other "test" that determines whether they can move to the next level in their educational or work career.

I've been doing this myself for years. I remember the funny looks I received when standing in the lobby waiting to be let into the room to take my licensing exam. Several people in my vicinity were sharing their fears. Our test had already been rescheduled due to snow, so if we didn't pass on this round it would be too late to schedule for the next round.

Yeah, I get that Anxiety and the other Inner Assholes would have a heyday with the thought that life might not roll out the way we planned (to get licensed as counselors and actually land paying jobs to do things like pay our bills and shit, oh and to actually help people like we wanted to be doing). However, I knew from experience that failing, even multiple times, was not the end of the world.

So I just started countering their fear statements. They would say, "If I fail today I won't be able to register for the next round," and I would reply, "Go ahead and register for the next round and then cancel if you pass." They would say, "What if I can't pass... ever?" to which I replied, "No one will care how many times it takes you to pass. Just go in planning to fail. Plan to set the record for most times failed." After a few more what ifs and my responses, they mostly stopped talking (while they attempted to figure out whether I was on drugs or just a lunatic) and we were soon ushered into the exam room.

I took the exam, staying mostly calm, and calling on my inner guidance the few times I noticed my anxiety ramping up. A few weeks later I got the notification that I passed.

My client who got fired was a Senior Vice President for a large company. He was already questioning whether his values were a match for the company culture—one of those situations where the company's Values and Mission Statement were not matching up with what a bunch of older white dudes in the C-Suite were actually doing. He and I had already talked about a possible exit strategy. It just happened sooner than imagined or planned.

My client was okay, though. Actually better than okay. In his words, "I'm so grateful that we were already working on my mindset around this. Thanks to the work we have done I actually feel pretty calm and can see this as an opportunity. Even my ego and inner critic haven't gotten too wound up about it!"

Exactly! When you know that you are in charge of your Inner Assholes, even getting fired can simply be an opening for your next opportunity!

Failure is another one of those parts about life that we do not like and do our best to avoid like the plague (or COVID). It's also one of those parts that is oh so important to learn to deal with.

The secret to innovation is allowing yourself to fail.

Did you know that there is a company called "X" that pays its employees to fail because it knows that if we constantly monitor ourselves to avoid failure then innovation cannot occur? Success hides in failure and yet our society has built quite the narrative about how failure is almost worse than death.

So when you are truly ready to turn those Inner Assholes into Allies, you will have to deal with failure.

How do you face your fear of failure? Plan to fail. Practice failing. Pick something and do the worst job possible. I tricked myself into writing this book by planning for it to be the shittiest book possible. If you are reading this, I'm going to say that it worked!

"What if no one reads it?" asked my ever so helpful Inner Assholes. "Who the fuck cares!" was my ever so empowered reply.

The only place where what other people think and do is important is in our narrative, the story we tell ourselves.

EMBARRASSMENT WON'T KILL YOU

The only person that I have shared this gem of knowledge with who wanted to argue with me was my tween. She reported that someone at school knows someone who knows someone who died of embarrassment. Instead of arguing with her (like she wanted) I chose to be impressed that she actually heard some of what I said and repeated it at school. Thankfully it's (mostly) the positive stuff and I have yet to be called into the principal's office for her having used my favorite word in an inappropriate place!

As much as your Inner Assholes would have you believe that embarrassment is akin to death, it is not. Period. It's just a way for them and society to keep you in line. Do you want to be a *sheeple*?

Consciously choosing to be uncomfortable and risking embarrassment is a huge step in getting ALIGNED with your Inner Assholes. When you choose to move in the direction of what you *want* instead of letting them dictate all of the restrictions and reasons that you "should" not, that's when they start to get the message that they are no longer the dictators in your life.

What if you could laugh at formerly "embarrassing" situations? Can you imagine how much more empowering that would feel?

What helped me to reframe "embarrassing" to "empowering" was to remind myself that laughter is medicine, so when I fuck up and it makes others laugh, it's almost like I'm a doctor. Can you earn your doctorate in humor? Sign me up!

ENTER HUMOR, STAGE LEFT

Now I was born curious and I bet you were, too. Being curious is a driving force in learning to use your eyes (we get curious about our own hands and learn to track them), your ears (turning toward sounds), your feet (walking), and your hands (oh, the things we seek to touch). Somewhere along the line, we turned our curiosity to safer things like Reality TV shows! Bring back your curiosity and put it to work at noticing how your Inner Assholes behave and how you can influence that behavior in a way that works better for both of you.

I was not born with a sense of humor. (OK, I was, but it took longer for me to nurture and develop it.) I was born with RBF (resting bitch face) and was often described as "intense" as a child. My father, on the other hand, always had a joke at the ready, and often they were "off color." I have more recently embraced how important it is to bring humor into my life and the lives of others.

Ever wonder why the Dali Lama giggles so often? It's like he is in on the Cosmic Joke! When we can take a step back, even sit back, and see the humor in both the big and little things, we invite our Protectors to also take a step back and become aware that most of the things they are "warning" us about are not actual life-or-death scenarios.

I recently attended a two-day seminar entitled "Integrating Mindfulness, Compassion, and Forgiveness Practices into Psychotherapy." Damn, that was a mouthful!

This particular seminar was both validating (as I already infuse mindfulness in my life and work) and inspiring as I could see the value in going deeper into this work for both myself and my clients.

Part of what was validating about this seminar was the point that, like the stoics, we can all benefit from thinking about death (ours, in particular) on a regular basis.

Are you squirming just a little (or a lot) right now? Wondering how we got from talking about humor to talking about death? I promise I'm coming back around to meet that one.

In general, those of us who live in developed countries do not engage in death-related *anything* on a regular basis. But countries that do take a more stoic and death-focused approach to life score higher on happiness and overall life satisfaction than we do here in the U.S. They score higher by a lot, actually.

It seems the more civilized and developed we as a society think we are, the more we seek Comfort and Certainty. With that goal as our pursuit, we delude ourselves into believing a fantasy to keep from dealing with the cold hard truth: None of us gets out alive.

Put down the remote, delete social media apps, and make it a priority to do the stuff that scares you.

It is also in this delusional state of pursuing happiness and success without dealing with our own mortality that Fear and Anxiety (and other Internal Assholes) gain traction. The next thing you know there is just this constant hum of Anxiety present under the surface, a feeling of crawling out of your skin, and potentially a whole heap of avoidance going on in your life.

So how do you embrace the process? Start dealing with the shit that scares you while using humor as one of your tools.

Pain, death, discomfort, embarrassment, failure... can you name any others? How do you decide to deal with the scary shit of life rather than avoid it? Choose to make practicing a priority!

Put down the Ben & Jerry's and the remote, delete social media apps from your phone, and stop doing all the shit that is not yours to do (hello, laundry and that report for your colleague) and pick up some passion and purpose. They are in there, but your Inner Assholes may be sitting on top of them.

David Carbonell, PhD, aka "The Anxiety Coach," introduced me to the important role of humor in the process of dealing with Anxiety. It applies to all of your Inner Assholes. In his book *The Worry Trick*, he shares how to Acknowledge and Accept the worry (sound familiar), then Humor It, before you get back to the Activity you were doing before it showed up. He calls this method "AHA." I love his examples of ways to bring humor into your mix and often read his haikus or sing his sample songs.

Speaking of embarrassing, the fact that I can get myself to sing in front of clients exemplifies that I have done some deep work in getting ALIGNED with my Inner Assholes. (My daughter would be mortified as she assures me that I, in fact, cannot sing.) Please imagine me now singing the following lyrics[3] to the tune of "Camptown Races":

I'll go crazy, then I'll die,
Doo dah, doo dah.
Panic gonna get me by and by,
Oh, doo dah day.

Make my head feel light,
Make my heart race all day,
Run stark naked through shopping malls,
Doo dah, doo dah day.

Here's the thing, your humor and my humor may not even be close to the same; however, don't let your Inner Assholes

---

3 Dave Carbonell. *The Worry Trick* (2016). New Harbinger Publications Inc: Oakland, CA (p.147).

talk you out of exploring this important step in the ALIGNED process. Humor is a great way to interrupt the pattern and habit of worrying that caused your Inner Assholes to have such awkward and annoying social skills. Take back your power and have fun while you are doing it!

WALKING THE TALK IRL

Embrace the process. Embarrassment won't kill you. Enter humor, stage left.

My first phone conversation with Nathan felt like I was being interviewed for a job, and now that I think about it, I guess I was... the job of helping this highly intelligent, well accomplished, and life-fully-lived man to embrace the process of dealing with his Inner Assholes.

Nathan had been working with his physician for years in an attempt to figure out what was "wrong" with him. In the end it was determined that there were no physical reasons for his "attacks" and Nathan was doing his best to accept that his Inner Assholes (Anxiety leading the gang) were really just fucking with him.

Nathan had a great sense of humor, so we started our connection there and became a team rather easily. Now Nathan did like to argue, so he kept me on my toes!

I knew that the hard part would be getting him to use his humor to deal with his Inner Assholes rather than using it to avoid them. It took a bit of patience on my part and commitment on his. He found ways to practice being uncomfortable (like returning to places where panic had put him into some pretty tenuous positions). Nathan found himself embracing not only the process, but his life more fully again.

Several months after Nathan and I completed our work, I received a package in the mail. No return address, so I was a bit concerned. As soon as I opened it, though, I started laughing and had no doubt as to the sender. It was a bobble head of Slimer from Ghostbusters, Nathan's anthropomorphized Anxiety!

SUMMARY

Depending on where you fall in Camp Failure (for it or against it), this may have been quite the bumpy ride for you.

Let's review:

> Failure is not actually optional, it's imperative. Since actual success and innovation require failure, it's time to figure out how to embrace it!

> No matter what you have been led to believe, you cannot actually die of embarrassment. Make the shift from embarrassed to empowered by learning to laugh at your—you guessed it—perceived failures and fuckups.

> Humor is an essential pattern interrupter and is used to break your habit of worrying, ruminating, and giving power over to your thoughts. Use it wisely and often.

ALIGNED
ACTION STEP:

Choose an area where you know that you are overly intense in your life—work, home, friends, parenting, a hobby... someplace where your Inner Assholes are making you miserable, just sucking the joy out of your relationships with the people and activities that you want to enjoy, but aren't.

Now, get your creative juices flowing and find a way to infuse the situation with humor. Notice what shifts or changes. You can do this. I have faith in you!

Chapter 7 "D"

So how do you know when one of your Inner Assholes is telling you the truth versus when they are just fucking with you? You learn to Discern, or recognize, the difference between signals and noise.[4]

> **Discern** (verb)
>
> *1. perceive or recognize (something)*
>
> *2. distinguish (someone or something) with difficulty by sight or with other senses*

If you are stepping off a curb and your Spidey sense tells you that a car is careening around the corner... and you are potentially in its path... that's a signal. If you wake up at 4:00 A.M. with the question of whether you said the wrong thing to you coworker (friend, boss, mother-in-law, that kid in elementary school) one day, that's noise.

Yes, I used a couple of extreme examples, but you are a smart cookie and can extrapolate the evidence here. Most of what gets a rise out of you via your Inner Assholes and their obnoxious thoughts (which are usually accompanied by obnoxious feelings) is noise. Practice noticing that. *Discern* is a verb, so take action here.

---

[4] Thank you to Reid Wilson and Lynn Lyons for presenting this process of discernment and the vocabulary to distinguish.

> **Discernment** *(noun)*
>
> *1. the ability to judge well*
>
> *2. (in Christian contexts) perception in the absence of judgment with a view to obtaining spiritual guidance and understanding*

Discernment, however, is a noun and what I find interesting is that the second definition specifically references Christianity. I am less concerned about specific religion here as I am curious about how the definition points out the importance of "absence of judgment" in the perception of (fill-in-the-blank). That's the ticket! Your Inner Assholes heap on judgment like jam on toast. Learn to Discern by leaving judgment out of the equation!

So how do you take thoughts and feelings (which, if you remember, are not facts) out of the discernment process? I like to think of it as shifting into neutral. Your thoughts and feelings are important, they just don't allow you to access your wise mind as easily as you might think. Shifting into neutral is getting to the place between logic and emotion, where your answers actually lie.

Sounds simple enough, right? It is simple, once you commit to practicing it regularly. Just like any other new concept that you want to create a new habit for, you have to break it down into bite-sized steps and then keep practicing until you wake up one day and know that you own them!

I love those light bulb moments that clients have when they realize they own a new habit, usually one they have been practicing for a couple of months, and we celebrate the success that their effort has awarded them! Going from "I don't know" and overanalyzing to "I can see clearly now what my options are" is powerful stuff!

DECIDE

Decisions suck, am I right?

But why do they suck? Because you are caught up in all the shit that your Inner Assholes are spewing at you, and instead of being in the moment, you are attempting to be 10 steps ahead like it's a game of chess. Even chess masters are not 100% accurate at predicting the outcome of a game. Why do you think that you can make the "right" decision every.single.time?

Remember back in Chapter 4 when I shared that during a time of great decision fatigue a wise counselor taught me the trick of just picking any decision, and then if that path was not working for me, I could make another decision? Yeah, do that!

Pick a path, and if it doesn't work, then choose another one!

Of course you aren't satisfied and want more details, don't you? Your Inner Assholes have you convinced that it cannot be that simple. OK, here's some more information for you to chew on. Let's talk about Values.

Getting ALIGNED, not only with your Inner Assholes but with your Values, helps in the decision-making process. Instead of factoring in a bazillion different (and often opposing) pieces of information—which is bound to bind you up tight—ask yourself which choice is in alignment with your values.

If your Inner Assholes continue to berate and scare the shit out of you to the point of overwhelm, then go back to Chapter 1 and get ALIGNED with them before you make a decision. Being in decision fatigue is not going to help you make the best decision for you; it is going to lead you to making a decision that may be influenced by cognitive bias and overwhelm. In other words you will be making a decision from a place of emotion rather than logic.

Which part of your brain—the emotional part (when it is on overload) or the logical one (when it is not clouded by your overloaded emotional brain)—makes the best decisions for you?

We love to assume that we are logical creatures, but alas, we are not. Our best decisions do have a basis in logic, but our emotional reactions to our Inner Assholes' inter-pretations of what is going on around us keeps us from accessing our logical brains.

Do your best to remember that feelings are not facts. Take the deepest breath you can, exhale fully, and then access your logical brain. If you are struggling with this, you can actually trick your Inner Assholes by playing a moderately challenging game (one that requires you to use your logical brain) for a couple of minutes and then go back to your decision. Now that your logical brain is part of the process, you will find it easier to determine a path that is best for you in that moment.

DEAL WITH IT (OR DELEGATE IT?)

The number #1 challenge that folks who are Anxiety Sensitive face is learning to "deal with it."

No, I don't mean "shut up and just fucking deal with it." I mean using all that you have learned about how your Inner

Assholes (Anxiety, Inner Critic, Impostor, and your loud VoD) work, and facing them head on until you are the boss of them!

No more hiding, avoiding, or cowering to their demands!

In an ideal world you could wave a wand and make all of the discomfort that your Inner Protectors cause go away. We do not live in an Ideal World so remember that those Protectors do have an important job to do. You know, they keep you alive!

So the sooner you give up the fantasy of a life filled only with certainty and comfort, the sooner you can actually get in the driver's seat and live your life. Yes, it's messy and uncomfortable at times. It's supposed to be. If you didn't get dirty, you didn't have fun! Yes, I hear you asking, "But how do I flip the switch and do this differently?" Excellent question!

First let's determine whether you tend toward a Fixed Mindset or a Growth Mindset.

I discovered these terms (and the theory behind them) while reading Dr. Kelly McGonigal's *The Upside of Stress* and Carol Dwek's *Mindset: The New Psychology of Success*. Both of these great resources focus on how the stories we tell ourselves about the "bad" parts of ourselves and life are what cause our suffering, not the aspects or events themselves. This lines up with Byron Katie's work as well. It's not what is actually going on within or around us, but rather the story we (and our Inner Assholes) tell ourselves about it... our perception.

Being open-minded is not the same as having a Growth Mindset. You can have a Growth Mindset in one area of your life and a Fixed Mindset in another. The good news is that no matter where you start, you can change.

So what does this have to do with contemplating death and transforming your Inner Assholes into Allies?

Everything?

None of this work is possible if you are not open to embracing change and believing in your ability to grow and evolve.

If you have a Fixed Mindset and are not willing to budge, it's likely that you will just continue to see your world through a narrow lens and allow your Inner Assholes to keep leading you around by your nose. Ouch, that sounds painful!

Believe in your ability to grow and evolve!

If, on the other hand, you can see a glimmer of hope (or some serious shiny rays), then you may be ready to embrace your Growth Mindset and make a major shift from being at the mercy of your thoughts and feelings to being in charge of your inner family members and get them to work more harmoniously!

Human beings (with the exception of those like Buddhist monks who spend four hours or more meditating each day) suck at being able to see the big picture. More often we spend the majority of our time caught up in our own bullshit and believing everything our mind, via our Inner Assholes, has to say.

What's my point? Basically it is "get your head out of your ass" and notice what's going on around you. Make a conscious decision to take charge of your life and get your

Inner CEO to demote your IAs, then get them to work for you rather than against you!

Now, lest you think I am saying that you are to give up all of your worldly possessions and live a life of service to others, I am not.

That "jump to conclusions" thing you just did is part of Anxiety's cognitive distortion of all-or-nothing thinking. Dealing with the ups and downs, ins and outs of life does not require you to live the life of a monk or priest or nun or whatever you think of when you think of sacrifice.

"Deal with it" has more to do with making a conscious choice not to avoid the messy parts of life. Stop overdoing to evade the uncomfortable feelings associated with your kid not getting their science project done, keeping up with the Joneses, getting your boss's kudos (but not a raise), attempting to do it "all" in your business, or any of the other million things you do daily that keep you from actually answering the question, "What's the fucking point?!?!"

The point is that you have one wild and precious life. If you choose to spend it avoiding your messy feelings and letting your Internal Assholes run your show, well, is that really living the life you imagined?

WALKING THE TALK IRL
Discern. Decide.
Deal with it. (Or delegate it.)

Diane was a Superstar with a clear vision to build a business for an underserved population in the mental health field. Intelligent and a risk taker, she brought her dream to fruition through her own blood, sweat, and a few tears. She built bridges and a kick-ass team for her business. We connected, though, when Diane realized that she had made it to the top, but found it pretty fucking lonely up there!

Diane checked off the boxes for High Functioning Anxiety, Inner Critic, and Impostor Syndrome as her trio of Inner Assholes. During our work together Diane uncovered how having her hands in all of the pots was actually managing rather than leading her team and business. She did the work to discern when her IAs were demanding that she control "everything" and how to get them to back off and let her Inner CEO make the decisions. The better she got at discerning and deciding with her IAs now being Allies instead of Assholes, the more she found ways to free up her own time to be more creative and to enjoy her success with less stress!

Oh, and that loneliness factor that many superstars face? Diane realized that other colleagues her age just wanted to pick her successful brain, and her Impostor told her that she didn't have enough age or experience to reach out to other superstars. With me behind her with my fancy compassionate ass-kicking boots, Diane got over herself and started reaching out to other successful people in her industry and made some very valuable connections. Her Inner Assholes no longer get to keep her to themselves!

SUMMARY

Discern whether your Inner Assholes are actually giving you valuable information or if they are just fucking with you.

Stop letting your IAs in on your decisions. When you put their opinions aside, remember that feelings are not facts. When you make decisions from your logical brain that align with your values, you will find yourself making decisions like a pro.

Dealing with your IAs does not have to be all-consuming or even drudgery. You have walked through all of the steps necessary to get ALIGNED with those parts of yourself that don't cooperate easily with your vision of how things "should" be. Thank them for giving you the opportunity to look at life differently and move forward with a more empowered way of thriving.

ALIGNED
ACTION STEP:

If you are not clear on what you value in life, then I suggest doing a Google search for a list of values... then pick your top 3. This will go a long way in supporting yourself when you have a decision to make. Simply ask yourself which choice aligns with your values.

Last and definitely not least, here is one of my favorite "tools" for dealing with the struggle that often ensues when attempting to transform your Inner Assholes into Allies: Dump Journaling. If you have struggled with unlocking the magic that comes from journaling (like I used to), here's how to Get Over It. One of the main reasons I have found for why people don't journal is simple: they buy beautiful journals and then their Inner Assholes dictate that "shit" is

---

not allowed to be written in them! The work around? Buy (or find at the bottom of your junk drawer) the most basic, nondescript, even "ugly" notebook you can find and then dump all the shit that your Inner Assholes throw at you in there. Just write. No editing. No judging. No should-ing. Just fucking write and then don't go back to read it. It's for dumping, not for creating or inspiring. Just dump the shit and walk away. Your mental load will be lighter for it!

Burrito (Wrap Up)

From Acknowledgement and Acceptance to Decide and Deal With It, you now have all of the things you need to be ALIGNED with your Inner Assholes. (Or at least a whole lot more than you did before you started on this journey with me!)

So are those IAs feeling less like assholes and more like allies yet?

Teaching our Inner Selves new social skills takes time. You have time. Use it well.

Remember that your Anxiety, Worry, Voice of Doubt (VoD), Inner Critic, Impostor and any other IAs you identified truly are doing their best to protect you. Are they overdoing their "job"? Yep. Getting rid of them is not a choice, so stop trying so hard to avoid or annihilate them. A better use of your time and energy is to get ALIGNED with them and start enjoying your success with less stress.

What is one step that you are willing to take today to let those fuckers know that you and your Wise Mind are in charge and that they are allowed a voice, but not a vote?

If you haven't done the Action Steps at the end of each chapter (I know I often don't), I encourage you to go back and pick one and do it. See how that feels. Then do another one and see how that feels.

Changing your relationships with your Inner Selves is similar to working on and evolving the relationships that are important in your outer world. It takes time, energy, and commitment. It is also messy, imperfect, and frustrating at times. You know what else it is? Worth it!

Writing this book for you was definitely a wild ride for me. Imagine a car with me in the driver's seat and a bunch of Assholes dressed up like clowns shoved together in the back. Lots of bitching, moaning, threats, and shit being thrown at me while I attempted to navigate this road. Was it a picnic? No. Was it worth it? Hell yes! Now go forth basking in your Belief Relief and with your new way of seeing your relationships with those inner parts of yourself that previously tripped you up and stressed you out.

If wrangling your Inner Assholes by yourself feels like too much of a challenge, I'm here. One of my favorite things is to throw a lasso around a wild IA and teach it how to work with you rather than against you!

I invite you to reach out to me at lynn@lynndutrow.com or visit the website at www.lynndutrow.com and get 25% off your enrollment in ALIGNED, my signature six-pack of sessions so you can wrangle your Inner Assholes and start enjoying your success with less stress.

ADDITIONAL RESOURCES

Michael L. Bennett and Sarah Bennett, *F*ck Feelings: One Shrink's Practical Advice for Managing All Life's Impossible Problems.* Simon & Schuster, 2015.

Brené Brown, *Atlas of the Heart: Mapping Meaningful Connection and the Language of Human Experience.* Random House, 2021.

_____, *Braving the Wilderness: The Quest for True Belonging and the Courage to Stand Alone.* Random House, 2017.

_____, *Dare to Lead: Brave Work. Tough Conversations. Whole Hearts.* Random House, 2018.

_____, *Daring Greatly: How the Courage to Be Vulnerable Transforms the Way We Live, Love, Parent, and Lead.* Avery, 2015

_____, *Rising Strong: How the Ability to Reset Transforms the Way We Live, Love, Parent, and Lead.* Random House, 2017.

_____, *The Gifts of Imperfection: Let Go of Who You Think You're Supposed to Be and Embrace Who You Are.* Hazelden Publishing, 2010.

David A. Carbonell, *The Worry Trick: How Your Brain Tricks You into Expecting the Worst and What You Can Do About It.* New Harbinger Publications, 2016.

James Clear, *Atomic Habits: An Easy & Proven Way to Build Good Habits & Break Bad Ones.* Avery, 2018.

Stephen Covey, *The 7 Habits of Highly Effective People: Powerful Lessons in Personal Change.* Free Press, 1989.

Ralph De La Rosa, *The Monkey is the Messenger.* Shambhala, 2018.

Glennon Doyle, *Untamed.* The Dial Press, 2020.

Carol Dweck, *Mindset: The New Psychology of Success.* Ballantine Books, 2007.

Michael Easter, *The Comfort Crisis: Embrace Discomfort to Reclaim Your Wild, Happy, Healthy Self.* Rodale Books, 2021.

Elizabeth Gilbert, *Big Magic: Creative Living Beyond Fear.* Penguin, 2016.

Adam Grant, *Originals: How Non-Conformists Move the World.* Penguin Books, 2017.

_____, *Think Again: The Power of Knowing What You Don't Know.* Viking, 2021.

Sarah Knight, *F*ck No: How to Stop Saying Yes When You Can't, You Shouldn't, or You Just Don't Want To (A No F*cks Given Guide, 5).* Voracious, 2019.

Mark Manson, *The Subtle Art of Not Giving a F*ck: A Counterintuitive Approach to Living a Good Life.* Harper, 2016.

Hara Estroff Marano, *A Nation of Wimps: The High Cost of Invasive Parenting.* Crown Archetype, 2008.

Kelly McGonigal, *The Upside of Stress: Why Stress Is Good for You, and How to Get Good at It.* Avery, 2016.

_____, *The Willpower Instinct: How Self-Control Works, Why It Matters, and What You Can Do to Get More of It.* Avery, 2013.

Michelle Obama, *Becoming*. Viking, 2018.

Martin N. Seif and Sally Winston, *What Every Therapist Needs to Know About Anxiety Disorders: Key Concepts, Insights, and Interventions*. Routledge, 2014.

Kim Scott, *Radical Candor: Be a Kick-Ass Boss Without Losing Your Humanity*. St. Martin's Press, 2019.

Ron Seigel, *The Extraordinary Gift of Being Ordinary: Finding Happiness Right Where You Are*. The Guilford Press, 2022.

_____, *The Mindfulness Solution: Everyday Practices for Everyday Problems*. The Guilford Press, 2010.

Dr. Claire Weekes, *Hope and Help for Your Nerves*. Berkeley, 1990.

Reid Wilson, *Stopping the Noise in Your Head: The New Way to Overcome Anxiety and Worry*. Health Communications, Inc., 2016.

Reid Wilson and Lynn Lyons, *Anxious Kids, Anxious Parents: 7 Ways to Stop the Worry Cycle and Raise Courageous & Independent Children*. Health Communications, Inc., 2013.

Sally M. Winston and Martin N. Seif, *Overcoming Unwanted Intrusive Thoughts: A CBT-Based Guide to Getting Over Frightening, Obsessive, or Disturbing Thoughts*. New Harbinger Publications, 2017.

Valerie Young, *The Secret Thoughts of Successful Women: Why Capable People Suffer from the Impostor Syndrome and How to Thrive in Spite of It*. Currency, 2011.

ACKNOWLEDGMENTS

With thanks to my cousin/friend Jennifer, for holding me up when I kept thinking I was falling.

To Petchy, for making me look good.

To Demi, for making me sound good.

To Leigh Anna, for being my technical backup.

To Jana, for the constant reminder of the customer journey.

To Julie, for capturing my spirit on film.

Thanks to my family for supporting me even when I didn't know I needed it.

And thanks to those who helped fund this project through Kickstarter. My deepest gratitude to all for your support of my shenanigans!

Elise Abromson
Laren Anderson
Melissa Anzick
Susan Au
Sarah Barber
Alicia Barmon
Barbara Barry
Mona Thomas Bausone
Amy Beal
Lila Beall
Terrie Bentley
Martha Boenau
Jennifer Boidy
Dulcie Bomberger
Zoe Brittain
Jennifer Burkhardt
Stephen Cagle
Dahlia Cain
Helene Toney Cain
Becky Campbell
Lisa Campbell
Krista Cappelletti

Barbara Cardone
Tony Checchia
JoAnn Coates-Hunter
Teresa Cochran
Stefanie Cox
Bonnie Davis
Heather Davis
Naomi Davis
Michael DeHart
Donna Delaney
Cassidy DeMos
Carrie Dennison
Janine Dimitriou
Stephanie Duncombe
Sarah Eddleman
Elizabeth Felgate
Caressa Flannery
Rebecca Flores
Sally Fulmer
Deborah Galvan
Maia Gemignani
Sara Gemmell

Emma Geraghty
Leigh Anna Geraghty
Mary Gibbons
Maren Good
Amber Gouge
Kai Hagen
Kristin Hamrick
Mike Hansell
Julie Hanson
Kim Harmon
Julia Hattershire
Rose Heather
Sheila Helmick
Jim Hochadel
Dami Hunter
Cory Johnson
Nancy Kay
Amanda Keating
Krista Kilbane
Melissa Kovatch
Jana Krizanova
Kenny Lebherz
Laurie Leonard
Kim Levy
Marjorie Lewis
Caitlin Lindsey
Tali Llama
Jennifer Lolli-Hall
Laura Long
David Luu
Cyd Maubert
Meredith McAdam
Sherry McCoy Quinones
Lisa McCrohan
Sara McGarvey
Sarah McNicholas
Leslie Moore
Deborah Morrone
Nancy Mudd
Kerstin Neuper
Thea Orozco
Evelyn Pacitti

Jennifer Padilla-Burger
Anjali Pattanayak
Molly Pelzer
Kimberly Perlin
Melissa Persaud
Solveig Petch
Andrea Poteat
Elan Poteat
Ann Quasman
Malissa Radonovich
Lawrence Ramstad
Laura Reeth
Sarah Reuland
Lauri Rhinehart
Lori Leitzel Rice
Laura Rippeon
Carolyn Robistow
Teresa Russell
Sarah Santacroce
Chelsea Saul
Jamie Dee Schiffer
Christina Sieren
Cassie Simpson
Djohariah Singer
Elizabeth Smith
Kara Smith
Cheryl McDonough Snyder
Demi Stevens
Joe Stine
Lera Straits
Karina Sweeney
Bri Swyter
Betsy Tobin
Michelle Tolison
Kortney Trevino
Megan Vandersluys
Jennifer Walker
Melissa Lajeunesse Ward
Wes Warner
Mike Wizbicki
Elizabeth A Woodward

Made in the USA
Middletown, DE
19 October 2022

12960841R00076